Hope I
Hardship

By

Ronnie D Stevens

Preface

Who am I? I am just a random guy you don't know, who has written a book. I had previously always put all my thoughts, feelings and emotions into my music. Then I realised that I wanted to reach a different audience. I'm not arrogant enough to think people would care about my life per se; but I have good reason for sharing my story, which is hopefully to help someone else who has been through some hard times. Whether that be trauma, grief, heartache, physical pain, or general mental health issues. I have been through a lot for someone who is just turning 40. I have witnessed many people struggle. Some didn't make it, including close family. Luckily for me, I managed to turn adversity into fuel. But believe me, it hasn't been easy. I nearly didn't make it myself. Every day is still a battle. I hope there is someone who can resonate with my journey. If one person comes up to me and says thank you, your book helped me, then mission accomplished. That is what this is for. If you have been kind enough to purchase this book, then from the bottom of my heart, thank you! You may also like to hear that a substantial percentage of the proceeds will be donated to a carefully selected animal charity. I was going to select a mental health charity, however us humans have a voice and finally, mental health is being taken seriously. Plus, I still love dogs more than humans! Sorry! If there is one thing you can take away from this book, it is to never give up and to believe in the process. No matter what anyone tells you, keep fighting!

Chapter 1

The Darnley

I was born in 1984, and I am positive I wasn't "planned". I'm not sure how many parents want another child sixteen years after they had the last one. Especially with my mum being on the wrong side of forty and my dad being on the precipice of fifty! I'm assuming there was a malfunction, but I'm here now.

Growing up in the mid-to-late 80's was certainly a different time; I can recall as far back as 1988 or thereabouts. I was the youngest of three, with my brother David and my sister Tracey being much older than me. As aforementioned, David was sixteen when I was born, and Tracey was eighteen. And I know now that wouldn't have been ideal for them. A bouncing new baby boy is soaking up all the attention and love. I never really contemplated that before, literally, until I just wrote that last sentence.

Firstly, I'd like to try and brood over a few positive memories. Before I dive too deep into the underbelly of trauma that was my childhood, the pub I grew up in was The Darnley Arms in Cobham Village, in Kent. It was a huge playground for me, I would scurry around and play freely alone. Completely encapsulated by my own company, playing with toy cars or a football to pass the time. I used to help Dad do the bottling up in the morning. I would earn my beloved 50p and go to The Candy Box and buy my sweets, a shop I would go on to live in; but more on that later.

Under the bar in the Darnley Arms, I remember there being an old hi-fi, I used to plug a microphone in and sing when no one was around. I distinctly remember the song; it was My Girl by the Temptations. This memory is so vivid in my psyche because only the week before I had experienced my first kiss behind the central pillar of the pub. All whilst my parents were busy drinking and talking at the bar. I have never told anyone this and I find it hilarious, that one I recall, and two, I was a little romantic at heart at the tender age of five. I can't remember the girl's name right now. I do remember her brother, Bradley, as we were best friends back then. The woes of a broken-hearted young boy who hadn't even started primary school yet.

Tracey and David were grown-ups at this point, I was effectively an only child. My mum Megan and dad Ron were always busy, so more often than not, I had to source my own entertainment. I found this extremely easy, due to no lack of imagination and curiosity - much to the frustrations of my parents sometimes! Looking back now, I fully understand. I'm not resentful towards them for not being available for large parts of my adolescence; they did everything to keep clothes on our backs and food on the table.

One of the things I found to entertain myself, was to pick up bad language I would hear either from the bar, or my brother's bedroom. Mainly ones that consisted of four letters. I'll let you fill in the gaps. So, who would I be not to apply those four-letter words? I must have candidly thought to myself as a five-year-old boy. So, that's what I did one afternoon. I proceeded to walk up and down the stairs and say the words. And I quote: "Fuck it," "fuck it," "fuck it" over and over again. I recall there were a lot of stairs, at least into double figures. And I said "fuck it" on every step. I'm not certain how much I walked up and down those stairs. My guess is plenty! I still find this funny in 2024. A mere 36 years later. You're probably wondering now. How did you stop? Well, I remember that very moment all too well. It was abruptly brought to a grinding halt by my mum. She grabbed me, slapped my arse, dragged me to the bathroom as I was crying, then shoved soap into my mouth, and screamed "DON'T YOU DARE USE THAT LANGUAGE IN MY HOUSE!" These days, that could be seen as child abuse. I'm not sure an eyelid would have been batted back then. Regardless, lesson learned.

Two things I cherished dearly as a child were my dogs, Sam and Toby. However, I was too young to understand that riding them around the pub like I was going into battle wasn't acceptable. I still feel guilty for that to this day. I now understand how wrong it was, as they were both so old, bless them. Nevertheless, they had a good life regardless of my antics and lived well into their teens. R.I.P. to those beautiful boys. There were only a handful of nice, significant and memorable "funny moments" that I can look back on fondly.

My dad and I were walking the dogs out the back, on returning, we passed my brother David's shed, where he would be constantly tinkering around with his motorbikes. He would sit and talk with all his friends. I think I was around five or six years old. I opened the door and for some unknown reason, picked up a Stanley knife off the floor and told them all to stay where they were, or I'd stab them! They all cracked up laughing, David included. Unfortunately, my dad wasn't so impressed. Needless to say, another slapped arse and proper bollocking. I can't say it wasn't warranted. My dad had to set an example and make me aware of the dangers of knives. A slightly harsh but needed lesson in my youth and blissfully unaware little mind.

Living in The Darnley, I discovered I was pretty handy with my fists. My mates, Arnie and Craig, who were brothers, used to come to the pub with their dad. While our parents were drinking, we'd be outside playing. We were as thick as thieves, doing everything together. Constantly building camps and running about climbing things. Getting up to all sorts of mischief. Another boy named Stephen used to come to the pub with his dad. None of us liked him. He was an outcast and always tried to muscle in on our fun and annoy us. One day, Craig hit him. It wasn't like a serious punch to the face, but a good enough warning. Craig said to his younger brother Arnie that he could beat Stephen up. Despite Stephen being significantly bigger, Craig was right. Arnie ended up doing just that, not too long afterwards.

I was never one to initiate a fight. I hated confrontation and still do now. If I can avoid it, I will. It's as soon as someone lays hands on me that things change. I'm quietly confident Craig may have instigated Stephen and I to fight. Craig seemed convinced that even I could take Stephen. Despite my small stature, Craig egged me on to fight him. I didn't want to, and I tried to avoid the situation if I am being honest. Craig grabbed Stephen's hand and pushed it into my face, I lost it. I jumped on him and started swinging. As I said, it was kid violence—nothing vicious or dangerous. I took him down comfortably and thought to myself "I'm quite handy" in my little head. Which later turned out to be true, much to the detriment of my primary school life. But we were all kids, having a scrap, climbing trees, throwing things around, and playing football. Nothing out of the ordinary.

We were all up for causing trouble in the village. We certainly weren't popular in the mid-to late-'90s. Another pleasant memory of my younger years was when I used to sit at the bar on a Friday night after school and share a bottle of Holsten Pils with my dad's employee and close friend, Russell. I'd tell him about my week, the problematic times, and how hard life was at school. He drank most of the bottle. It was my first glimpse at adulthood and how to hold a "decent" conversation at a bar. You can't shut me up now; so, it must have worked!

Thinking of myself as that six-year-old child, I was full of mischief and curiosity. I suppose all kids are to some degree. It's strange some of the things I seem to be able to recall from such a long time ago. Such as, one of my brother's friends, Damien who had fake front teeth, I never knew why? He used to scoop them out of his mouth with his tongue and show them to me. I remember sitting there in utter disbelief! Like, how was he doing this? It must be magic! I tried for hours to scoop my two bottom front teeth out of my head, to no avail. I can still remember sitting on the edge of his bed, asking him how he did it, and repeatedly trying over and over again—the naivety and innocence of youth.

The last of my good memories from those days was my sister always taking me out whenever she could. I think that was when she kind of became my mum. At the time, I was completely unaware of how important she would become in my life. You're probably thinking, of course she is important to you, she is your sister! But you will understand much later in the book just how much. Despite her driving an old clapped-out Y reg Fiesta at the speed of light, frightening the living shit out of me through the narrow lanes of Cobham, she was and remains the most important person in my life. I suppose that is where I can draw a line under the somewhat good memories attached to my prepubescent days. As I approached seven years old, things started to take a turn, for the worst. There was a tension throughout the living area in the pub that filled me with dread. I knew, even then, that something was awry. I just didn't know what. There would regularly be shouting and screaming. Whether that be from my siblings' rooms or my parent's upstairs.

Although The Darnley was my playground during the day, it was my nemesis at night. The loud, thumping music and bellowing voices from the pub echoed throughout my room when I got sent to bed. I can still clearly remember being terrified to live there. I feared that some drunk would come wondering up from the bar and find me and whether if I screamed anyone hear me. I lived in constant fear. I didn't know how to verbalise it without my parents' just telling me to stop being silly and go to sleep.

My room was on the second floor at the back of the pub. You had to walk through my mum and dad's bedroom to get through to mine. It was a weird living area, there were three floors to the pub, with Tracey and David's rooms on the top floor. Every night my parents used to come up with some of the staff and our dogs to say goodnight. I remember Margaret (a bit of a battle axe) and Catherine, a very tall, beautiful blonde lady. They both kissed me goodnight, I'm sure they did that to reassure me. It was quite sweet thinking about it.

One particular night, my parents had just put me to bed. I was feeling brave and hung my hand over the side of my bed to deliberately scare myself. For a kid who was already petrified, this wasn't the best idea. I'm sure many of you will probably relate to hanging your foot out of bed to see if there was a monster going to grab it and quickly put it back under the covers. Cause we all know nothing can hurt us when we are tucked under the quilt. My hand was dangling by the side of the bed, to my absolute panic-stricken horror, something walked past the side of my bed. It was big furry and brushed my fingertips; I wasn't dreaming! I screamed at the top of my lungs, I mean, it was blood-curdling. So much so, that my dad and others flew into my room within seconds (I guess they can hear me after all). They hit the light on and found me firmly pinned with my back against the wall, white as a sheet, shaking and screaming inaudible gibberish stuttering "monster, something furry". As I looked across my room, Sam, our dog, walked out of the bedroom. My parents had shut him in as they left and didn't realise. Although that was a welcome relief, it played on my mind. I slept with my back against the wall from that day on, and you bet I made sure my mum and dad checked that room thoroughly before they switched the light off, every single night without fail. The nights were ever so lonely for me, harbouring that innate feeling of fear coursing through my veins when I went to bed. It was debilitating, I can still remember how paralysing that fear was.

I had a box of toys and teddy bears under my window that I started to almost fixate on, maybe to make myself feel better? I had a couple of toys that made me feel a bit scared. I sound like a wimp now, I'm sure. One of the toys in question was a lion that used to sit upright with piercing black and orange glass eyes. And this strange clown, he had striped pyjamas with white cuffs, including a striped hat. He had a flesh-coloured face, hands and feet like a human, sewn-on blue eyes with black pupils, and bright yellow straw-like hair. His body was material, not solid. I used to stare at him, wondering if he would come alive. As I say, vivid imagination. This led to a very unusual and recurring nightmare. I would turn into the clown in my toy box and begin flying around in circles in my room. I'd do three laps and then get sucked into the door handle. It was like a portal to another world. I landed on the other side where three witches were waiting for me, gathered around a cauldron. One of them was stirring away, looking at me menacingly. She would say, "You're

7

never going back to your parents, you live here now." I'm not too sure how long this lasted, but it felt like years back then. In the grand scheme of things, it ended up being the least of my worries.

Things never really improved at home, there was still this tension and rigidity in the atmosphere between the family. I only found out later why that was. It turns out my brother David had major issues. He would regularly steal money from my sister's room and be horrible to her. He'd also been stealing from my parents, which later came to blows in the most horrific of ways. I'm not sure how long he had been doing this, but it must have been a long time. My parents were doing okay for money. The pub was always busy, and we had everything we needed. My dad spent his hard-earned money on lavish gifts for David, hoping he'd start behaving. But it was counterproductive.

My dad was a lovely guy who tried his best. Despite what I am about to tell you, don't let that change your mind. It comes full circle, I promise you. After many, many months, maybe even years of David thieving money from my parents, it got too much. My dad couldn't prove it was him, however, he decided to start setting traps for David to fall victim to, to catch him out. The pub was hemorrhaging money; they needed to find out why. How could a once successful business all of a sudden be failing? So, my dad sat down one day and devised a plan. He used to do the cashing up and remove the till from downstairs, then transfer all of the money into a large suitcase every night and slide it under his bed. After monitoring the staff and regularly checking the tills throughout shifts, he knew his staff were clean and had to start looking closer to home.

After a lot of deliberation and stress, he started to think that maybe it was being stolen from his room at night. My parents were notoriously deep sleepers, and my brother David took full advantage of this. He'd been sneaking into their room weekly to take a load of cash and coins out of the suitcase to fund his drug and gambling habits. He'd quietly unzip the suitcase, take what he desired, zip it back up and made off with the cash. Once my dad concluded this is what was happening, he set the trap. A trap

8

that would catch David red-handed and change our family dynamic forever. My dad could have just waited for my brother and caught him coming in, but instead, he wanted to outsmart him and prove a point. One that meant David had no way to wriggle out of. So, my dad decided to cut open all of the pound bags and put a thin line of Sellotape to cover the holes to give them a temporary fix. With it being in the pitch black of night, my brother would never have noticed this modification. Eventually, David would return to the suitcase, which was to be the last time ever. Unbeknownst to him. He took multiple bags in his hands and started to sneak out. Then, much to his surprise, CRASH!!! A bunch of pound coins smashed onto the floor. My dad turned the light on and said, "I knew it was you! I just wanted proof; I want you out of this house tomorrow!"

I was fast asleep and had no idea what had gone on. My sister Tracey may not have known at this point either. We sure found out the next morning. I remember hearing loud screaming and shouting. I came out of the front room to see what was going on. It was my dad and David having this blazing row. My mum stood in between them to try and split it all up. It boiled over BIG TIME. My dad worked his fingers to the bone seven days a week in that pub. He gave us everything we needed, and my brother still wasn't satisfied. I don't know what my brother said or did to him in this argument, but whatever it was, it went too far. My dad snapped; they began wrestling on the floor. David was beckoning my dad to hit him, so he obliged. I mean, he fucking hit him. My mum jumped on them to split up, which was now a full-on fight, although David didn't retaliate. My sister Tracey took me in her arms and tried to get me away. A six-year-old boy watched his dad and brother have a full-on punch-up on the landing. Screaming, shouting, punching, swearing, and crying all happening in front of me.

Despite Tracey's best attempts to protect me from seeing what was going on, it was already too late. I had witnessed the entire scenario before she managed to intervene. Once my dad stopped hitting him, my brother got to his feet, screamed at him, and told him to fuck off! He ran down the stairs of the pub as my old man

9

threw him crash helmet at him and told him not to come back. I can still play this scene over in my head to this day, like it's forever burned into my brain. Down to the most insignificant little details - where I was standing, the carpet I was standing on, the colour and pattern on my brother's crash helmet, where everyone was fighting. It never left me, and it never will. I think when you experience such trauma at a young age, it sticks with you for life, doesn't it?

It must have been horrible for Tracey as well, at the age of only 23, completely powerless and unable to do anything about the situation. She held on to me in the hope that it would stop. That event broke me as a child. Afterwards I wasn't the same. Through what I had witnessed, I had become what the doctors said: "very likely to be permanently damaged". I developed a stammer, my hands and feet turned inward through sheer fear. My mum and dad took me to the hospital where they said there was a high possibility I'd never walk or talk properly again. I would trip over my own feet and fumble my words for up to 12 months afterwards.

Luckily, I did make a full recovery (physically), but mentally, I would never be the same. There was no operation to realign my feet, as it was something I wasn't born with, they didn't know if my feet would return to normal again. They recommended that I wear my shoes on the opposite feet to straighten them which did eventually work. Although I can't quite remember how I started talking normally again thankfully I did. Unfortunately, not long after my recovery David reappeared. I'm not going to lie; I was upset that he came back. The house was so much more peaceful without him being around, my parents, Tracey and I were living in harmony, and I was dreading it going back to how it used to be. I cried and said to my mum that I didn't want him back; he scared me. He'd always show off in front of his friends and hung me by the ankles over the landing stairs until I cried. I remember the day he returned. I was crying on my mum's lap in the front room. I am pleading with her to make him go away. He walked in and said something—I'm not sure what—but I yelled at him to fuck off! I'll never forget it. A six-year-old me, completely distraught, inconsolable and ravaged with fear. David slammed the front room door and stormed out. I can't remember if he ended up staying or not that day. I think my parents made him go soon afterwards, because of how much I was impacted by what I had witnessed, and they couldn't have their six-year-old son living in terror like that. I felt guilty that I had pushed him out of the family home, and if truth be told, I never really forgave myself.

I know it may seem crazy to think a 40-year-old man still feels guilty for that, but what was to come will give you more understanding. Anyone reading this book would likely sympathise. Looking back now, that seemed to be the final nail in the coffin regarding pub life for the family. It became clear that my mum hated it anyway. She never enjoyed working in the kitchen; my dad loved the pub game; he was very much a social creature and entertainer. Being behind the bar and having his friends come in weekly for a drink and a chat was great for him, but it was time to move on.

Shortly after all these horrendous events, The Darnley slowly started to dwindle. What was once a busy pub, became quiet and almost desolate. There were two other pubs in the village, which were situated on the main road within a quarter of a mile of each other, making competition high. Money was tight and the pressure on my parents' marriage was building. Tracey ended up moving out with her boyfriend, who ironically is called David. All whilst I was living in constant anguish, thinking, at any moment, my brother would come busting through the front door again.

All my friends lived in the village, and I went to school there. I didn't want to move far away as I loved the area. Mum and dad were very cautious about what to do. I know full well that I was at the forefront of their minds when deciding where we were going to live. When they shared the news with me that we were moving to The Candy Box, I was overcome with excitement. Moving to my favourite sweet shop was a dream come true. The relocation was perfectly timed; the new home was much smaller, but there was more than enough room for the three of us. I was so excited; I could barely contain myself. I couldn't wait to get in there and eat lots of sweets. What kid wouldn't? It was much-needed good news and helped lift my broken spirits. When I was at school; I couldn't stop daydreaming about moving into the shop. All my friends were jealous and eager to visit my new home. They probably thought they'd have free sweets too, bless them. I mean, so did I! Unfortunately, that wasn't the case. Dad had to make this business work after my brother David almost single-handedly sank his last one.

On the day of the move, I was getting ready to go to school, when mum said to me with a beaming smile, "Don't forget, when you come home tonight, we will be in the shop". I'm not sure if she was happy, they had a shop, or relieved she was out of the pub. Probably a bit of both. I trundled off to school; buzzing from head to toe. Something must have happened at school that day, because I completely forgot what mum had told me that morning. It baffles me how I could have forgotten the only thing I had to look forward to. I left school and went back to The Darnley on auto-pilot. A woman I didn't recognise answered the door. I asked for my mum and dad, and, for a moment, I thought, "Have I been abandoned"? She screamed, "You don't live here anymore!" I ran to the shop, crying my eyes out. Turned out she was an evil old bitch that woman. Mum consoled me and said, "I told you we were going to be here, silly". I could tell my parents weren't happy with how the woman shouted at me. I think she was dealt with. Verbally, of course.

Chapter 2

The Candy Box

We were finally in the shop; I felt a huge sense of relief. Eventually, a morsel of happiness. Things moved quickly and my parents opened the shop with immediate effect. The owner lived next door; he wasn't the nicest guy in the world. He came across like he thought he was better than us and looked down on our family. When I became older and got to know him, I had his card marked. Even at that young age, my uncanny knack for understanding certain character traits was natural for me. Despite him in the background, it was starkly better than before, and ultimately, I was free from the pub. And free from my brother David. We had a lovely, long garden I could go and play in, even though it was a much smaller playground for me. I felt safer there and more content. Although, deep down, I knew something was missing. I concluded that it was a dog. I had never known any different and always had dogs throughout my childhood. I pleaded with my mum and dad to get another dog. I desperately missed Sam and Toby; who both had passed over the rainbow bridge before we moved to The Candy Box. When our dogs passed over it hit my dad hard as he was there for their final moments. Not only that it was like he had lost a limb, Sam was my dad's shadow. He followed him around that pub and never once left his side. He'd lay behind the bar when my dad was working, if dad moved, he moved that was non-negotiable. So, when Sam passed on, it hit my dad. I'd never seen him cry like that before, he wept, as we all did. Sam was a beautiful soul and pretty much my dad's guardian angel. If you're wondering what about Toby, he was Tracey's little shadow in very much the same way.

A few weeks later my dad received a phone call. It was Brian, my parent's accountant and dear friend. He knew we'd recently lost the two dogs, but he had a major issue on his hands. Brian was a short, slightly plump elderly gentleman. He had wispy grey hair on the sides but was bald on top, much like me now - minus the grey. He had a bulbous red nose, rosy, red cheeks and was the gentlest soul. He was such a lovely man that was always kind to me. He was so genuine; didn't have a bad bone in his body. He'd always give me a pound when he came around and spent time talking to me. Brian was also a dog breeder. He bred Golden Retrievers and Springer Spaniels for forty years. He was a well-respected man. Extremely well thought of in that field, as well as in his profession. I remember being told by my parents that the higher-society types would contact him for puppies. Well, you've probably guessed where this is going by now. I will never forget Brian; I wanted him to be featured in this book. As they say, you die twice in life: once when you physically leave, then again when someone says your name for the last time. And although I don't want to be the last person to say his name, he's still in my thoughts and is fondly remembered.

Anyway, back to the phone call. Brian trepidatiously said to my dad: "Ron, I wouldn't ask you if I wasn't desperate. But, in forty years of breeding dogs and homing them, I have never, to my knowledge, made a bad call. Until now. I have heard that the family I recently sold a puppy to is being badly neglected. I have to get him out of that house ASAP!" Brian then solemnly said to my dad, "I can't have him myself due to circumstances and there's no one else that I know could have him. I know you've just lost Sam and Toby, and believe me, I wouldn't ask if I weren't in dire straits". My dad said "I can't right now, Brian. I am honestly not ready". It was less than a month after losing Sam and Toby. Brian said "OK, can you at least go and look at him, Ron?". My dad owed Brian after all the years he had helped him with his accounts. My dad being a man of integrity and principle, agreed. I overheard all of this and was like a Jack in the Box, absolutely convinced that, we were getting another dog. Dad reigned me in sharply saying "Whoa, easy, son. We're only going to look at him". I lowered my head in quiet hope as I carried on playing with my toys in the dining room.

Fast forward a day or two, and we were on our way to Gillingham to go and see the dog. We pulled up at this house and knocked on the door. The man who answered seemed nervous and a bit standoffish. His eyes were sunken and as black as onyx. I straight away felt a bad vibe exuding from him. We entered, and immediately, I felt like I did at The Darnley. There was an unhealthy atmosphere in this place. I didn't like it; I wasn't overly concerned, as all I cared about at that moment was the dog. Where was this dog? He ran past us and hid under the coffee table. As he catapulted through their dining room, the young girl of this couple slapped him on the back. She could have only been about three or four years old at most. I thought it was weird, but I was just turning eight myself. I almost nonchalantly brushed it off. I walked over to the coffee table, where the dog had run to hide. My dad warned me to be careful. The dog was as close to the wall under that table as you could physically get. It reminded me of the time when Sam got locked in my room that night at The Darnley, and I was in a similar stance. So, I knew he was terrified. I wanted so badly to stroke him. He was eventually coerced from under the table by the man. Who, for reference, is going to be known as (cunt) from this point on. I know that's not a popular word with some, and I promised myself I wouldn't use it in my book. But I think it's a completely justified tag for any grown man who beats an animal.

The dog was shaking and appeared cautious. As I stroked him, he crouched to the floor. I looked at my hand afterwards to see a clump of hair in my left palm. I'll never forget looking at him and thinking, why are you such a skinny doggie? And I will never forget counting his ribs. That may seem bizarre, but as a kid, I couldn't compute why I could see them. My old dogs didn't look like that. Within less than ten minutes, my dad said sternly, "Give me the lead mate, we're taking him" Although this guy was bigger than my dad, he got that lead pronto! The guy's wife was lingering in the background, barely present. Their little girl was next to her. I wanted to be happy, but I recognised this feeling of impending doom all too well - it transported me back to the pub once again. We got my new doggie into the car. You'll never believe what his name was. Sam!

We made our way home to The Candy Box, where he would have a good life. He was only 16–18 months old when we rescued him. Even though he had a traumatised puppy life, he would go on to have a good adult one. Dad called Brian and told him the good news. Brian was so happy that he came over only two days later to see him. I don't want to dwell on Sam's old owner, but I do want to say that years later, we found out some horrendous news. Six months after we rescued Sam, he got put inside for beating his wife. That's the sort of scumbag he was. A pathetic, weak man and a bully! Hopefully, the guys inside gave him a good shoeing. Anyway, back to my new doggie, Golden Sam, beautiful golden Sam. He was naughty at the start. He kept nicking my toys, I told him off. My dad explained that he did this because he knew no different and had never had love and attention. That I had to be patient with him. I immediately felt guilty and hugged him. Sam was very shaky and nervous for months. Understandably so as well, poor thing. But after lots of love and training, plus some well-needed nutrition, he came out of his shell. He was a playful and happy dog within six months. He had a one-of-a-kind personality as well. Sam loved human company. He was everyone's friend.

Our next-door neighbour, Vic the Jeweler, as he was known (sounds like a character out of Snatch, now I've written that down!) Anyway, I digress. Vic once said to me that every time he walked out of his shed, Sam leapt up at the wall to be fussed. Vic saw him as a big golden lion looking down at him. This made me laugh. It was a much-needed intervention to have Sam join our family. Especially for me, it was fresh hope at the time and that feeling of safety I so dearly missed from having a dog in the house.

Things seemed notably better between my mum and dad, and now that we had the dog, I felt a sense of reprieve. The shop was so much more relaxing to live in. I didn't feel constantly on edge. Everything finally seemed to be "normal." All my friends wanted to come over because of the novelty of their mate living in a sweet shop. It was like the coolest thing possible at that age. I would still spend hours alone playing with my toy cars on the landing upstairs, it was my favourite thing to do with my time. I would pester my dad and ask him every day. "Dad, which one of these cars is faster?" I'd line them up. I made him put them in order. I'm positive this did his head in, and I am just as positive now that he didn't have a clue. Nonetheless, he made the effort, always got involved, and gave me the answer I craved. I would then remember the order, go upstairs to the landing, and create two teams of Matchbox cars. If you are over the age of 30, you'll know what they are. Then I would play Bulldog with them. My imagination has always been good, and later on, near the end of this book, you'll see it come into play in the most unpredictable of ways.

Life was nothing, even remotely similar to what it once was in The Darnley. Although, I could still feel an unease between my parents. It was now (1992) Tracey decided to, once again, save me from the uninviting undertones of home life and take me away for the weekend to the Isle of Wight. Something in particular sticks out in my mind. We visited a place called Alum Bay. The home of coloured sand. As soon as I walked in, I remember being captivated by the multi-coloured sand that surrounded me in this little hut-like building. Tracey asked me to pick a small glass-shaped vase to put the sand in and make a present for my mum. I remember being baffled; all the different coloured sands stacked upon each other. Then the lady offered me this pin to put through the middle to make it have this wavy effect. I initially refused, as I couldn't understand how each layer of sand wouldn't collapse and ruin my good work. She convinced me in the end, and I was mesmerised by it. It broke my young mind at the time, but the result was amazing. I was chuffed with my little vase of sand and couldn't wait to present my mum with it when I got home. That little trip had a huge impact on me; I was a happy young child again.

My sister Tracey was always present and would continue to visit us regularly. David was only sporadically around. But even he seemed different, he was a little more content, so I thought anyway. Even though things seemed notably better than they were, I knew there was still something wrong with me. I'd lash out very quickly and have one hell of a temper. I still possess that to this day. I keep it under lock and key because I'm an adult now and in control of my emotions. It's reserved for special occasions these days. Unfortunately, that temper bled over into my school life. I attended Cobham Primary School, just up the road. Although there were noticeable improvements to home life, school wasn't the same. I used the school as a place to vent my anger and frustrations. I don't think my mum and dad were aware of my temper until my godmother Ella, who worked at the school saw me fighting one day. I will never forget the words that my mum later relayed to me: "He fights like a grown man. It's not normal. Meg". I was pulled to one side by my parents and told not to behave in that manner. Unfortunately, those words of concern fell on deaf ears of a now nine-year-old young boy.

Anger is the easiest emotion to display, and I think it was from the trauma that it manifested itself. I would regularly fight with a kid called Daniel. He'd always pick on me, and I'd always be happy to oblige and punch him square in the face without even a flicker of thought beforehand. You upset me; I would punch you in the face. Sometimes, not even a warning, just straight to violence! I suppose it was seeing what I had at such a young age and not understanding how to express myself that led to these actions. As a nine-year-old kid, I was psychologically damaged and confused. It was the only way to unleash it. Daniel finally, after a few beatings, got the message. I mean, I don't regret it at all. Sitting here now, if someone deliberately starts provoking me, pushing me, or trying to coerce me into a fight, I'd probably do the same now. Albeit, once given someone a fair warning and a chance to change their mind. Strangely, many of the games in primary school revolved around some sort of violence. At break times, we would wrap our school jumpers around our heads, leaving peepholes for the eyes, and pretend to be Ninja Turtles. It was our class against another. Somehow, it always involved someone getting hurt. Rarely myself or my friends.

Reflecting on this it was like I went from the scared kid at the pub to someone who quite a few of the boys at school were at least wary of. The Ninja Turtle game did throw up some casualties of war. A big lad, Benjamin, from a year or two below, decided one lunch that he thought he could take me down. After I hit him with a sweet right-hander and knocked his tooth out, he quickly evaluated his choices soon after. I'll never forget him scurrying about all lunch, looking on the floor for his tooth so he'd get a pound from the tooth fairy. It was after that day that I knew I could fight. So, I did. Too often as well. I never liked the initial confrontation of a fight. The build-up stages of all the name-calling, pushing, and shoving. But, once it got going, I flourished. I possessed this fearlessness and absolute refusal to be beaten. I don't have that quite as much these days. But I still partake in controlled violence, to a certain degree. Ironically, it would go on to be my saviour.

I just never learned my lesson in primary school, despite the requests of my godmother Ella and parents; it just seemed like it was a calling. On this particular day, my mum walked me to school. When we arrived, I was in the cloak room, hanging my coat up. She was just holding onto my lunchbox while I did so. Daniel must have forgotten my previous message. He came wading in, elbowing everyone, and he hit her in the chest. She gasped in pain. That was it; I went for him. He looked at my mum and me and realised what he had done. She stopped him to make him apologise and told me not to react. There was no chance of that. I was hellbent on revenge. No one touches my mum, whether it was by accident or not. From a very young age, I have always been fiercely protective of the people I love. And I'm still the same today. I'd give my life for theirs.

That whole morning, I could only fixate on Daniel. I couldn't take my eyes off him. I kept looking at the clock for break time and then looked over in his direction. He knew he was in trouble, as soon as the bell went, we all went outside to the playground. I had one thing on my mind, and one thing only. And that was to fill him in for hitting my mum. I walked over to where he was sitting under the Conker tree and unleashed on him. I'd never hit

19

him more than once or twice before. This time, I got him with three solid punches to the face. The whole right side of his face was bright red and bruised. Job done! The onlookers in my year took note, I'm sure. Daniel was crying and beaten. I felt great about myself, not going to lie. He kept his distance from me for some time after that and reigned it in.

The kids who regularly displayed the sort of behaviour like I did, would do so, because they weren't academic. But that wasn't the case for me. (At least in primary school.) I was near the top of my class for reading and writing, and I was half-decent at all the other subjects outside of art. Thank God I can write, I certainly can't draw. That's my sister Tracey's forte. I enjoyed most of the lessons in primary school. I often liked to complete tasks and try to do my best in all subjects. Don't get me wrong; I wasn't a brain-box, but I was no dummy either. It helped that I was noticeably happier living in The Candy Box. Despite not demonstrating behaviour to suggest so. I wasn't actively looking for fights, but they always seemed to find me.

There was a tight-knit group of us at school in those days. There was Arnie, the twins David and Paul, Robert, and myself. We would all play 40/40 and bulldog most break times. Which always ended up with someone crying. No matter what I did it seemed some form of trouble came as a byproduct. Around this time of my chaotic and wayward behaviour, a new girl joined the school, two years below me, called Lizzy. We instantly hit it off. Arnie, my best friend, also hit it off with her too. We quickly became the three stooges and caused nothing short of absolute mayhem in the village. I'd just reached year six and was now the big fish in the small pond. Well, I say big fish. I was still 3 feet tall, but that never played a factor in growing up in any way. We would all meet up after school and go terrorise whoever we could. Lizzy and her family lived in The Ship, only a few hundred meters from The Candy Box. We all spent loads of time in The Ship and wore big coats so when we went to the back of the pubs storage unit we could slide beers up our sleeves. Afterwards we would go to the fields and get drunk at the tender age of 11.

Lizzy was the youngest of three, like myself. Her two older siblings were Patrick and Jenette. So, in that regard, it was a similar situation. Despite the fact that her brother and sister were around her age, we would all go out together in the woods and build camps or jumps for our pedal bikes. When we got bored of that, we would take to throwing things at cars, knock down ginger, or stealing milk off people's doorsteps. It was a tiny village with not much to offer children. So often we'd be getting in trouble. We also worked out a way to break into The Cricket Club on Sundays. I'd jump on Craig's shoulders, because I was the smallest and most willing. Then I'd climb through a window and go and open the door. We would try to syphon beer from the taps if they left the bar area unlocked. I was so easily led and did anything that my friends would do. That's not to say that I didn't initiate the trouble either. I just didn't know how to say no! That inability to say no also landed me a 16-year smoking habit. Yep. I started smoking at the ripe old age of eleven. Unfortunately, being easily led went on to land me in serious trouble only months later!

When I stayed over at Arnie's house which was on Thong Lane, ten minutes up the road, his house backed onto Cobham Woods. We were out of sight and out of mind, honestly, some of my best days were had there. I hated having to go back home after staying over, I genuinely felt upset. I think it was because, deep down, I was lonely. Going back to The Candy Box was quiet in comparison. Arnie and Craig had all the cool things, like motorcycles, we'd go around the paddock on. We had so much room to play and do what we liked with our time. One of these things was gravely dangerous. We didn't understand just how dangerous it was until later in life. We were all in Craig and Arnie's garage one day, Patrick, Lizzy, and I were all chatting while Craig was working on one of his motorbikes. Patrick was sitting on it all of a sudden, he raised his head and went, "Oh wow"!!! He's like "everything's all flickery and fuzzy, it is amazing!" At the time, we didn't know what he was talking about. He had accidentally breathed in the fumes from the open tank on Craig's bike. The petrol had gotten him as high as a kite.

What was to follow could have cost one of our lives, and that's not hyperbole whatsoever. Once the realisation hit home, we all wanted to try it. It was the most incredible feeling, I won't lie. At the age of only 11, feeling like you're floating about buzzing with everything looking like a static TV from the 90s but in colour was surreal. I am pretty sure it was the school holidays. That made it even worse. We quickly made a habit of it, to the point where we were all addicted. Craig never really got involved much, apart from at the very start, Patrick kind of followed suit. But Lizzy, Arnie, and I didn't stop for months, and I mean months. It was out of control, but we were 11 years old and thought this cool feeling had no repercussions. It was harmless fun in our eyes. Oh, little did we know. It got to the stage where Craig asked us to stop, or he would grass us up. We didn't believe he'd ever do it, as Craig was no grass. So, we carried on with the attitude of whatever. A week later, shit hits the fan. In the most biblical ways for all of us. Craig held to his word and thank God he did. If you're reading this, Craig, thank you! You saved a life that day. If not mine or Lizzy's, your brothers. Needless to say, we were in for a huge bollocking. All of us got grounded for as long as they saw fit. We were not allowed to see each other again. I was in absolute floods of tears, stuck in my room for the entire summer. It was this moment that divided us and things were never the same. Our parents were concerned about us doing it again. They weren't going to take the chance, and knowing the severity of what could have happened must have scared them.

8–12 months later, Lizzy's family was to move to Surrey. I was distraught—literally inconsolable, for a while. Arnie and I fell back into being friends, and our parents relaxed a bit. We never sniffed petrol again, that's for sure. It wasn't long after that we were to join Secondary School. I was concerned that Arnie would go to a different school. But much to my delight, we both joined Axton Chase. Although, there were some monumental changes ahead which would affect both of our lives, respectively, in the next two years that neither of us could have ever predicted.

Chapter 3

School Days

Now, I'm not going to get too ambitious in this chapter. It will serve more as a prerequisite and segue into Chapter 4. Though I thought it was necessary to document some relatively "normal" moments of my life and reflect on being a young boy and doing what boys do. Starting secondary school is quite a milestone for any young lad; I was not an exception to the rule. Arnie and I joined Axton Chase School in Longfield. We had become close again. I think we were both a bit nervous deep down, eleven-year-olds coming from a tiny little village. Going from a small school of around 150 students to a huge school, that was home to well over 1,200 students, was daunting but we never spoke about it. We just cracked on and were back to being small fish in a big pond, and that is exactly what it was. A massive pond. Full of largely unsavoury characters. I must admit, I had a great time at Axton Chase (outside of lessons). Although home life wasn't great for either of us at that point.

Arnie's family had their troubles, and my family still had plenty going on. Not that I had any idea of how severe things were; my mum and dad were pretty good at keeping things from me after what went on at The Darnley Arms. I found it quite hard to adjust to secondary school life, I could not understand why all the teachers were so strict. Within six months, I was put on report. Which I stayed on for the best part of three years, as did Arnie. I was a bully and a truant, which I am still ashamed of. Bullies are the dregs of society and pathetic people, and I was one of them. Arnie and I walked to school together and had each other's backs. If you hurt me, he would hit you. If you hurt him, then I'm getting stuck in.

It was at the latter end of 1996; when my parents broke the devastating news, Arnie's dad had died in a motorcycle accident. We both took time off from school, I couldn't bear to see my mate in so much pain; I took on his grief wholeheartedly. It was months before he returned to school. I went back a bit before but struggled without him. He was my rock and he had been broken into pieces. I didn't know how to help him, there were no words of solace I could have possibly given him at that age. I just couldn't stand to see my best friend in pain.

As we both approached year eight, times were still tough. However, we were not the smallest fish in the pond anymore. We got a feel for the school and were a bit more confident. We also had a third wheel in the group - Adam. Adam was a spindly and geeky kid; your stereotypical computer nerd. Arnie and I took a shine to him, but we did pick on him a bit to be honest. It wasn't too malicious, for the most part. But he was still the brunt of most of our jokes, poor sod. We all smoked, so that was our way of being sociable. Behind the PE Hall was usually the designated area. One of us would "keep dog" as we used to call it. The others would have a puff on their snouts. None of us took school remotely seriously at this stage. Well, at any stage where I was concerned, and for good reasons that come into fruition later on. We just wanted to find any way possible to avoid work and be little gits. We had marked down specific lessons we would try to bunk throughout the week and go to the woods or into Longfield. We were all feeling down and had personal issues outside of school. I remember Adam was going through a tough time; it's not my place to discuss it in detail here. I think maybe that's why we connected though. We were all looking for a bit of escapism. Anything to take our minds off what was going on behind the closed doors of our family homes. All searching for a quiet void to drift off into and be left alone.

It was tough for me when things started to change once again at home. I noticed a shift in the atmosphere; not knowing what was causing it made me feel ill at ease. The honeymoon period of moving into the shop had worn off already and I was too young to have a grasp of what was occurring behind the curtains of my broken family. I must have soaked up so much subconsciously. I realise that now, as I would try to spend most of my time out of the house. Any opportunity I had, I would be outside, and that remains the same today. I love being outdoors and away from it all.

Arnie, Adam and I used to meet frequently outside of school. We'd go to Gravesend and get into all sorts of trouble in town. Throwing wet toilet tissue off the top of the Anglesea Centre at passing buses. Or pea-shooting people outside McDonald's, would also be a cheeky little highlight. Anywhere we went we caused mischief. We heard through the grapevine there was a youth club opening after school on Friday's. We decided to all join and that's where all the rules vanished. Longfield is now my playground. I had been promoted if you will. Things got so bad; everyone became almost lawless. It wasn't just us three. There would normally be anywhere between 15 and 20 of us, sneaking out of the Youth Club going on a rampage throughout Longfield. The residents had made multiple complaints to the school, it got out of hand to the point that it was brought up in a school assembly. It resulted in the Youth Club eventually being closed down because they couldn't police it.
It wasn't too long after this unwarranted behaviour, that I discovered a real passion for music. Which was a blessing in disguise, music gave me an outlet rather than being naughty. Back in those days, all the boys listened to Drum and Bass. I instantly became fond of it; you'd rarely see me without my Walkman. I would listen to the old tape packs I used to buy from the legendary Biting Back Records (If you know, you know). You wouldn't see me without my music today, I won't travel anywhere without my tunes. Mainly because of my undying love for music, but more importantly due to my recent discovery of having misophonia. I know now that music was, and still is very much another form of escape for me. It wasn't like I needed another excuse to tune out of school. I wasn't paying any attention anyway. I used to drift off, absent-minded, staring out the window, thinking of things I would rather be doing. The way I saw it, I had plenty of time for work; I could piss about for a few years at least. Well, that's what I thought anyway.

Unfortunately, not too long after that The Candy Box ceased to exist. Although we would remain living there. I was heartbroken; we couldn't compete with the shop up the road anymore. The best I could hope for was that we would live with little to no disruptions for the first time. It would still be just my parents, Golden Sam, and me. Maybe this could be the quiet my life needed. I don't think my dad enjoyed working in the shop. He didn't have the characters coming in like he used to in the pub and the social side wasn't there for him. My mum was indifferent to running the shop as well, from my recollection. It was another source of stress and a tougher business to keep afloat. Even without someone nicking every penny they made. Maybe it would be a blessing in disguise, my parents could have some much needed quiet in their lives for a change. That would be what I would tell the younger version of myself anyway. But what was to happen next bestowed anything but peacefulness upon our family.

Chapter 4

David

I would like to start this chapter with a fond memory or two I have of my brother David. He visited my parents' place for one night, on June 28, 1997. Mike Tyson was fighting Evander Holyfield at the MGM Grand Las Vegas. I remember David being noticeably chipper. The fight wasn't until 5 a.m. in the UK. Adam was over for the weekend, and we were determined to make it and stay up with him. We stole a load of fags off of him that night and David blatantly knew as well. We'd go into my mum and dad's bathroom and light them off with the electric heater and hang out of the window smoking.

At around midnight, we were all starving; David raided the freezer. We found a pack of Chinese ribs. My brother loved Chinese food. It was his holy grail of dietary requirements, so he bunged them under the grill to make us sandwiches. Roughly ten minutes go by until the grill is on fire! My brother is running through the kitchen shouting fire in the hole, flames billowing about two feet high. Adam and I were pissing ourselves, and so was David. There were a few casualties on the grill. Luckily, most of the Chinese ribs were salvageable.

We sat up for hours listening to David reel off funny stories from his past. I remember one where he went fishing with his mate, His friend was firing stones out of a catapult into this big Scottish bloke's swim, to wind him up. They were both drunk and to make matters even worse so was the big Scottish lad whom they were tormenting. This guy had had enough, stood up and screamed at both of them. "Get to fuck, ya fucking pricks." Dave and his friend were too pissed to care and didn't do much to calm the situation down. I don't think it ended badly, from my recollection. It was just a bit of harmless fun. I hold onto that memory dearly, almost like a picture. One that you have as a constant reminder, it warms my heart and still makes me chuckle to myself.

My brother David never really worked, not consistently anyway. On my birthday, he bought me a present for the first time. It was a front light for my bicycle. Now, I am quite sure that was 1997. David seemed to be in a good place at this time. I didn't ask why, or probably even thought to, at 12 years old. But that light meant the world to me. It wasn't anywhere near as expensive or grand in stature as the other presents I received that year, but it was my favourite present. By some distance as well, because of the sentiment. And do you know why I can place my hand on my heart and say that? Because that light is still in a bag in my kitchen, 27 years later. It was nice that we rekindled and developed our relationship. I know that he resented me and was struggling with the fact that I got all the attention from our parents. But for that year, it was like we made friends, and now I sit here and ponder, thoughts racing around my head. Jesus Christ! Oh, my god. He must have planned it all along. He knew he had to make peace with his little brother.

Six months fly by. It's December 1997. I hear my mum on the phone crying her eyes out. She was pleading with my brother. David had taken a serious turn for the worse. He wanted to come and live with us as he and his "girlfriend" had split up. David was in a bad place, I was looking at my mum, shaking my head in fear. Despite having spent a blinder of a year with him, he was back in his angry phase, I didn't want to risk it. Half a year of a good relationship still didn't repair all the damage done in the pub days. My mum wanted him home, but my dad refused and said no. I was constantly worried that he was going to come back home and for want of a better phrase, fuck everything up. It may sound like I didn't love my brother, but I truly did. I loved that man with all my heart, but he scared me, and I felt uneasy around him when he was angry. He could be violent, never towards me, but his temper was vicious.

I knew it was something serious when my mum started bawling her eyes out. I overheard her say "C'mon, David. Please don't be stupid; you can't do that". I was asking what they meant. They both knew deep down what was coming, I needed some warning. My brother was threatening to take his own life. I said "Don't be so ridiculous. As if he would do that". In the end, eventually, my dad gave in, they talked me around and said, just let him stay one more night. That night, he made his first attempt. Now, there are many people out there who would say he was crying out for attention. If you try to kill yourself, and you mean it, well, you succeed, right? Now, I'm not sure about any of you reading this. And I'm certainly not a doctor; but I don't know any man who could take 250 different tablets, drink a bottle of Jack Daniels and still wake up the next morning, do you? I found David, but I was blissfully unaware of what he had done. I thought he was drunk. I was laughing at him as my mum was shaking her head at me with fear and absolute terror in her eyes. David had woken up on the dining room floor, he tried to get to his knees but fell forward and smashed his eye open on the cast iron fireplace. Blood started trickling down his face. He looked grey and washed out; his eyes barely open. My mum sat in stillness. I could feel the energy from her being wrong.

My dad entered the room looking very angry. Russell, my old Holsten Pils friend, was in tow. I knew then that something was about to go wrong. Russell looked on edge, on high alert and jittery as he walked in behind my dad. They sat David down on a dining room chair. My dad was shouting at him, "I let you come back, and you do this in my fucking house. In front of your little brother. Fuck you!". Dad grabbed David by the collar and slammed him up against the wall. Russell quickly intervened and tried to calm the situation down. My dad was broken by all of this. He may still be coming across as a harsh father who didn't care. But, by the end of this book, you'll love him as much as many others did. It'll be nowhere close to how much I loved him.

David then dejectedly leaned forward to tie up his Caterpillar boots. My dad said, "Fuck your boots, just get out". To which my brother replied "I gotta have a bit of pride, ain't I?" That didn't go down well, and my dad went for him. Russell, once again, got in between. Thank God he was there. David was homeless and had nowhere to go at this stage. It quickly became apparent that he wasn't going anywhere other than the hospital. I can't remember what happened on the journey from our house to the hospital, but I do know David collapsed at some stage.

I never witnessed that moment and I am glad I didn't. My dad went to the hospital with him, and from what I can gather, I stayed home with Mum. It was a dark time; I still didn't know he had tried to commit suicide. I will never forget what dad later relayed to me when I was old enough, about my brother's first attempt at killing himself. Dad said he was with David the whole time until he regained consciousness. When my brother opened his eyes, he looked at my dad and said these harrowing words "I'm still alive, aren't I?". My dad replied, "Yes, son". David said, "Oh, for fuck-sake". My dad knew from that moment David couldn't have been saved from the inevitable. It wasn't a matter of if. It was a matter of when.

David was still in recovery but he had got released from hospital. I knew nothing about what had gone on. Everyone was protecting me because I was young. I am eternally grateful for how hard they must have tried to save their little boy from the pain. My dad was at a crossroads and didn't know what else he could do. They tried getting him help many times, but in 1998, it wasn't like it is now. I mean, go back even a decade. How often did you hear about men's mental health? There were specialists who turned him away because of a lack of money to pay for treatment. At this stage, the whole family was poor. Just how poor, I didn't realise. It would later come out in my mum's diary.

Dad turned to one of his friends William, who had a bed and breakfast in the village, he paid him to put my brother up for a few nights. Will said to my dad, "He can't do that here, Ron. I can't have it". My dad had already spoken to my brother and forewarned him not to try anything. Unfortunately, my dad's request fell on deaf ears. Two days later, he was getting my brother down from the ceiling. He saved him just in time. Then, another attempt came and if I remember this correctly, the belt snapped on him. Maybe it was fate. Maybe he'd realise that it just wasn't meant to be. That he'd see the signs, carry on, find help, and go on to live a great life. On the 2nd January 1998 my brother David was found dead. He had hung himself in his flat in Maidstone, Kent. He finally got what he wanted.

The disturbing details surfaced, David had rung his girlfriend up beforehand and said to her; "You don't know what you're going to find when you come back here, do you?". She thought David meant that he had demolished the place and ruined all the painting and decorating he'd spent months doing. But that wasn't the case. When she returned a little later with her dad. That was when they found my brother hanging from the ceiling. Her dad frantically tried to cut him down and release him. It was far too late. He was long gone. And this time, there was absolutely and unequivocally no mistake. David stood on a paint tin to get his neck into the noose. That paint tin was so small that he could have put his toes on the floor to save his life. If that isn't a man who doesn't want to be here, then I don't know what is.

On the day my brother passed I was at Tracey's house. Mum and Dad were shopping. The phone rings, my sister lets out a muffled cry of pain. After she put the phone down, she walked towards me. Her eyes were full of tears, her face full of pain and anguish. She just shook her head. I knew; I just knew. She threw her arms around me, and we cry, cry, and cry some more. We didn't say a word for ages. We couldn't. Then came the realisation that we knew before our parents. Only moments later comes a knock at the door. Tracey opened it sobbing, with me doing the same in the background. I can't possibly describe or recreate the pain I saw on their faces that day. But all I can tell you is; you will have to go a long way to see more pain than two parents who've just lost their baby boy. They dropped their shopping bags to the floor instantly and wept. That moment lasted forever.

My mum died that day. Not literally, but metaphorically. I haven't mentioned him yet, but my brother had a son. He's still knocking around somewhere and notoriously hard to track down.

31

I thought if I brought him up earlier, you'd all prejudge my brother. His son, who I won't name for privacy, was just over a year old when David committed suicide. He knew he couldn't leave it any later and have his son remember him. I am guessing this is where I have probably lost a lot of you here, and I am not surprised. How could a man leave his son? My brother turned out to be schizophrenic, topping that with addiction and other mental health issues, you have a real cocktail of disaster. That man was in so much unfixable agony, I can't even begin to explain. You might be thinking, how do I know this as I was only a kid when he took his life. Well, I'm in that same pain today. I know how to manage it now and can sympathise with it. But I'll tell you my truth later.

In mid-January, my family and I are standing over my brother's grave, throwing a rose on top of his coffin. As a 12-year-old boy in utter disbelief, watching your older brother get slowly lowered into the ground in a box is something you'll never forget. Unfortunately, that was just the start. Normally, once someone has been laid to rest, it gives you closure and helps you accept their passing. But when someone takes their life, you're left wanting the exact answers as to why? We know some of the reasons, which I won't divulge here. But I know there's something else, and I will find out what. I have 999 pieces to the 1,000-word puzzle. We all know how important the last piece of a puzzle is. Even worse is when you can't find it. But I have a rough idea of where to look.

The impact of David going the way he did became forever etched into our souls. It's not something anyone can change, and there's no point in letting it consume you. I've learned this the hard way, as it consumed me for many years, 17 years, to be exact. I woke up one day and made my mind up. David has been dead for 25 years. In the last eight years, I have been much more at peace with it. It took a long time to stop listening to the voices on the periphery and listen to my own. The common view is that it is a selfish act. I don't entirely disagree. However, there is a huge caveat to consider here. Is it more selfish for someone to end their own life because of the irreparable pain they're in? Or is it more selfish for all of us to want them to be here in that agony for our gratification? Just think about that for 5 minutes and come to your own conclusion. That may sound like I'm saying go and do it if you want to. But in the 1990s, mental health didn't exist back then, especially men's mental health. The reason I'm still here is because there's always a choice. There's always hope. These days there is help available that you wouldn't have had back then. In the last chapter of this book, I will give you hope, and I will give you a choice by sharing with you what saved me.

In the late nineties, as you would expect, I had significant time away from school. There was no way I could face it. Months went by, and I was still a broken mess. But I had no choice in the matter and had to go back to school. I'll never forget telling my parents to warn my form tutor and let my class know. Just to give me a bit of breathing space upon my return. I was a bit of a joker at school, and I still am that joker today. I didn't want everyone to think I was just being weird or distant. The first day back, I walked out of morning registration. My entire year is staring at me. I am looking around, like, what the fuck is going on. Why is everyone looking at me? What have I done? My mum, in her unclear mental state, had rung the school and told the headmaster to tell the entirety of year 9. It was my first day back, and now, not only did I have to try and keep my emotions in check, I had to deal with multiple kids coming up to me and giving their condolences. It sounds ungrateful, I did appreciate it. But I just want to keep my head down and suffer in silence. Many days after I went back, I got sent home. I just couldn't do it. School, in my head, at least, was already done. I had just over two years left. Those two years were already firmly written off in my mind. It was just a case of going through the motions at this point. I had developed this intense inner rage and couldn't control my temper. A hormonal boy on the verge of his teens is angry, frustrated, and bereft. Seeking vengeance almost, needless to say, I played up at school, I played up at home, and I didn't care about anything much anymore. Other than seeing my friends from time to time, to take my mind off it. Then, all of a sudden, six months later, Arnie's mum takes him out of Axton Chase. I got knocked back again. Things were bad enough, never mind without my best friend by my side. But it turned out to be a blessing in disguise because we fell out later anyway, as his girlfriend decided to kiss me one night. I got the blame, and that was that. Friendship over!

The family had been through it, and all of us were on auto-pilot. Tony and Ann, my parents' best friends, decided to step in and take us on holiday to Cyprus. Take our minds off of reality for two weeks. I was so excited! It gave me something to look forward to. The week before we're due to fly out, Adam came over to stay on the weekend. We were going down the Leather Bottle pub slide on our rollerblades. The owner had previously said not to do it, but we're kids, right? You say not to do something it automatically means do it. Kelvin the bar manager shouts "Oi!" and starts to chase us through the football fields. Adam and I bolted out of the back of the pub. Running on the grass with rollerblades isn't easy. I would highly recommend not trying it. We go through the first field and seek refuge in the park. Phew we lost him! We were panting, out of breath, and full of adrenaline. We take a seat and think we're in the clear. I decide to get up on the slide while wearing my blades. Adam remains seated.

Then, out of nowhere Kelvin appears angrily through the fence shouting "COME HERE!" He approaches Adam, grabs him by the neck, and starts slamming him up against the wooden fence. I stared in shock and disbelief. He finally stops, Adam is on the verge of tears and shaking like a leaf. Kelvin then tells me to get down. I think to myself he won't touch me because I live three doors up. Surely? He does the same. I'm not as scared as Adam; I'm contemplating punching him in the face full pelt. But he's a big guy and I'm a four-stone-wet kid. He finally stops. I am fuming and want to kill him. We all left the park, Adam is completely catatonic, and Kelvin is trying his best to get ahead of us and get home. I knew what he was planning. I turn around and say to Adam "Mate, I'm sorry. I am going to go ahead, skate home and get my dad". As I passed Kelvin, I could not quite believe the words that came out of his mouth. He dared to mumble the words. "Oh, by the way, I'm sorry to hear about your brother". I did not acknowledge him. It just made matters worse!

I was pretty nifty on a pair of skates, Adam not so much. I sped home and as I approached my door, I didn't even slow down. I hit it full-on. As I do, Kelvin just goes past my house. He must have sprinted. I go through my front room and smash the dining room door open. Russell is sitting there with my mum and dad. They all jumped and wondered what in the hell was going on. I smash through the kitchen, grab the biggest knife out of the drawer, and start making my way back, stomping through the house manically, still wearing skates. My dad and Russell bundle me to the floor and disarm me. I'm inconsolable, inaudible, and completely lost in a red mist. They couldn't get a word out of me other than "I'm going to fucking kill him" over and over again.

After a few minutes, my adrenaline drops, I verbalise what just happened. Adam turns up just as I am telling the story. My dad took me down there. I knew he wanted to belt him one, but the Cyprus holiday was less than ten days away. Kelvin cleverly went back on his property, which meant he had the upper hand from a legal standpoint. My dad gave him a verbal dressing down, a few pushes and let him know how lucky he was. Adam's mum, on the other hand, was incensed. At the time, I was only sure of a few things in life. One of those things was, don't piss Adam's mum off! There were serious ramifications. She was a lovely lady. I have very fond memories of her but if you crossed her, then it was game on! And believe me, Kelvin must have wondered what tornado walked into his pub that day. I don't think she hit him although I heard she came very close. She let him have it in front of the entire pub, full of people. I wished I was there to see him shrink like the pathetic little man he was. I don't think he realised how close to grave danger he was in. Narrowly escaping a good punch in the face, Adam's mum and stepdad left the pub. Once everything calmed down, the tension over the next couple of days slowly dissipates. Our attention then turns to the holiday again. Our suitcases are packed, and the wheels are in motion

Chapter 5

The Domino Effect

We are heading to Cyprus, it's a welcome distraction from everyday life. I'm not entirely sure how my mum and dad felt about it at the time. Or if it was what they needed. Regardless, they knew it would be good for me. When we arrived at our apartment. I opened the door, and the first thing I saw was a dead cockroach behind it. I have never seen one so big. This thing was wearing Timberland boots and a leather jacket, and probably had to pay rent. He was that huge! I didn't like creepy crawlies as a kid. I nervously stepped away from it and proceeded to explore the rest of the apartment. It was a really nice and clean, despite our unwanted guest. We had a lovely view from the balcony. Once we got settled in, we headed out to get some lunch. Although Cyprus was a beautiful country, I remember the streets being quite dirty. Certainly, in the part where we were staying. I was used to Spain, which was completely opposite. I was a little disheartened and remember wanting to be in Spain instead for a day or two. It turned out it was near bin day and the streets were noticeably cleaner after the rubbish collection.

The surrounding areas were much more picturesque, Ann and Tony had been there before and wanted to take us on excursions throughout the holiday. They planned the whole thing out well to save my parents any stress. I am very grateful for that; it was a nice gesture. There was talk of this big mountain that we were visiting. I wasn't expecting what was to come. I was certainly not good with heights at the time. Even flying out there, I noticed that I was a little fearful. It was weird because I never even thought about it before. Maybe, looking back, I was growing up and becoming slightly more aware of real-life dangers and the reality that things could go wrong.

When we arrived at the Troodos Mountains, I was slightly nervous. We got in the coach, ready for a long trip to the top. As we made our ascent, I vividly recall looking out of the window and seeing rocks falling off the cliff edge. The wheels on the coach were right on the precipice of the mountain. The whole way up, I was genuinely petrified. It was anything but a short journey. There were a series of stops along the way to view certain iconic tombs and places of rest. It felt like days getting to the top, but it was most likely a couple of hours. On the bright side, it took my mind off things. Despite that, it was a once-in-a-lifetime experience and one I won't ever forget. The views were unreal! Unlike anything I had ever seen before. The tour guides also did a great job of putting my mind at rest throughout the journey.

The people were lovely out there, welcoming and warm-natured. There was a bar directly under our apartment. I can't imagine Tony spotting that before we went! Most nights, we would go down there and eat. They always had some music or entertainment going on. There was one night in particular that sticks out in my mind. Everyone at our table was talking away and enjoying the evening, when out of nowhere, came this massive scream. All a bit startled, we turned around to see what was going on, a few tables across from us, the women all had their legs lifted in the air. One woman was standing on her chair, terrified, and all the guys were laughing their arses off. It was a cockroach running around the bottom of their table. It was late in the evening, so the entertainment had died down. Other than the table where all the commotion was coming from, we onlookers just stared over in silence. I will never forget the noise. You could hear this thing's feet as it scuttled around the table. That was when I lifted my feet. The only way I suppose I can transfer that noise from my brain into yours relatively successfully is in the hope that you have seen the film The Mummy. Remember the flesh-eating scarab beetles? Yeah, that was basically what these giants were. Mum and Ann were feet up the same as me, dad and Tony were near to tears with laughter with the other guys in the bar.

The days that were to follow, I noticed dad's behaviour wasn't normal. He was not his usual jovial and witty self. He was in and out of the toilet constantly. He brushed it off at first, but it carried on for most of the second half of the holiday. I distinctly remember him talking to my mum, I heard him say, "Meg, I don't feel right". It was his tone. I didn't like it. The way he said it, his voice had almost a shaky timbre to it, that I hadn't ever heard before. I picked up on the strangest things as a child, I never really took stock of it until writing this book. Now I'm sitting here looking back on my younger self through an adult lens. It's irrefutable that I disconnected from many emotions as a child. It's almost like I'd treat it like any other piece of information. I'd recognise it, internalise it briefly, then discard it once I understood it and not linger on it for too long. It's not like I lack empathy, if anything I take on people's pain too much these days. All I can put it down to is that I used it as a defense mechanism. This, in turn, made me realise why I acted like I did six months after we got back from Cyprus.

I was so upset that dad was ill. It's like none of us could catch a break! Mum was much like me—very vacant and hardly present. Nevertheless, it was better than being at home. When the last day arrived, we all felt reality creeping back in. We know we're less than half a day away from being indoors and having to start all over again. We boarded the plane, very subdued and quiet. I vaguely remember glaring out of the plane window on the way home, numb and disinterested in the view. Well, that was until the plane caught fire. That got my attention! Just when you thought things couldn't get any worse, I'm staring death in the face at 30,000 feet in the air. We were only 20 minutes away from landing. After I processed what was happening, I turned to my mum and quietly said, "Mum, the plane is on fire" she replied, "Shut up, Ronnie. Stop winding me up. You know I don't like flying". I said, "Mum, I'm not joking!" She said, "Oh, piss off, will you?". At that point, I had to physically grab her by the head and turn it to look out of my window. She immediately panics! Other people started noticing, only seconds later, the pilot instructed us to stay calm, that one of the engines had blown out, and not to worry. Yeah, people didn't hear the "don't worry" part of that sentence. If your plane is on fire and there's black smoke billowing out of it, panic is kind of a go-to emotion. The pilot then announces to us over the Tannoy that we will have to circle the runway and wait to land, so the emergency services could get there and be ready. That didn't make sense to me and it still doesn't as I write this. We stayed in the air for another 45 minutes! I remember our plane banking over the sea and the runway. Circling around and around. My dad's reaction to it was "don't worry, it's only one of the engines, there's another three" with a comical tone. Typical dad. I can laugh now that I'm not in a ball of flames out at sea. Although I am still scared of flying today.

When we were eventually coming to land, I remember seeing loads of emergency service vehicles chasing us down the runway. There must have been a good ten or more in transit. I was relieved beyond belief. I thought, great, let's get off, but they made us stay on the plane for nearly an hour to put the flames out. Another thing I still don't understand to this day. But everyone made it off alive, thankfully. There were a lot of traumatised people. I wonder how many of them would have flown again after that ordeal. It took me over a decade to get the courage to get on another plane. And you would think, what are the chances of anything going wrong again?

We leave Gatwick, all noticeably disoriented and quiet. I don't remember the drive home, but I recall getting back indoors and that sense of impending doom lingering in the air. That horrible proposition of being welcomed back to real life that most of us disliked. My dad was still not well and immediately booked an appointment with our local doctor's surgery. Roughly a week after getting back, he went in to see Dr.Woods. He was examined and diagnosed with IBS (irritable bowel syndrome). Dr.Woods prescribed him some medication. The rest is history, right? Months go by, and this medication isn't doing much to ease my dad's continued discomfort.

I have just hit fourteen, things at home have taken another nosedive. Tension is readily apparent within the home and once more I can sense the unrest almost daily. My dad goes back to the doctor to explain that the medication is not doing much and that he needs a second opinion. He gets referred to the local hospital. After further checks to eliminate the possibility of the sinister Big C. The results came back. My dad got called to go in for a face to face to discuss his result. He's then told that he had been a victim of a misdiagnosis six months previously and that he indeed has cancer of the bowel. They need to act immediately, as they have already wasted precious time. We were understandably all angry at the misdiagnosis that Dr.Woods had initially given. But what was done was done, and there was nothing that would change the fact that dad had a battle on his hands. We all needed to focus on the reality of the situation and get him the help he needed immediately. It turns out the specialist said that it was my dad finding my brother on his second attempt, or his actual death may have brought the cancer on via shock! The everlasting effects of suicide, which continued to perpetuate throughout my family.

A slight glimmer of hope appeared! We had good news regarding my dad's cancer, in that it was operable, but it needed to get done quickly! He was whipped in for an operation not too long after. Understandably, we were all very nervous, as luck wasn't a thing you would associate with my family, especially for the last 18 months. We all waited, overwrought and fidgety, hoping Dad would make it through the operation. The surgeon Dr Stewart came running out of the theatre and told my mum and sister something either of them could expect. They were then faced with one of the toughest questions I have ever heard anyone ask. With barely a minute to decide, "Mrs. Gollop, I am currently halfway through your husband's operation, as I have gone to remove the tumor, there is one directly behind it that is smaller. It didn't show up on the CT scan, as it was hidden behind the shadow of the larger one. You have two choices. I can remove the larger tumor and leave the other one in, and your husband will live for 6–12 months, there's a high chance he pulls through the operation. Or, I can do my absolute best to remove both today, but there's a fifty percent chance he dies on the operating table". The room fell into silence, Dr Stewart proceeds to explain... "Although, if he does make it, the cancer is gone, and he could go on for many years to come. I can't sugarcoat this. That is the cruel reality". My sister was also involved in making the call, and in unison, they both agreed to take the risk and try to remove the second tumor.

Dr Stewart did just that and performed a miracle in that room. I am forever grateful to him for giving my dad the life he rightly deserved. I'll never forget walking into that recovery room and seeing my dad there with all these tubes sticking out of him, looking pale and weak. It was tough for my young eyes to see, but where there are situations cloaked in pain and misery, one guy you could count on to flip that on its head was my dad. Even though he was under anesthesia, the first words out of his mouth were, "I got to walk the lion when I get home. You should try holding that fucking thing." He was referring to Golden Sam in his roundabout way. Bless him. After what happened with my brother only 6 months prior, this was all a bit much to process.

I went even further into my shell, to which I became very hard to reach. I didn't want to accept what was going on; I was only 14 years old. When dad came home, he wasn't himself, and it took him a long time to get back to his old carefree and joking ways. Neither of my parents were working, outside of Mum doing the odd cleaning job, money was tight, and times were once again getting harder. The rent was going up by the month, it seemed. The pressure was building, and things weren't letting up. There was little reprieve for any of us. Mum and dad were arguing quite a bit, and I knew something was on the horizon. I just didn't know what that would be. Then, one day, I overheard talk of us moving again. I wasn't happy at all. My friends were in Cobham, and I didn't want to go to a new place where I didn't know anyone. I didn't understand the severity of the situation we were actually in at the time. I would come to find out in 2018 just how bad it was. I dismissed the idea of moving immediately and didn't want to acknowledge it. From a young age, I buried my head in the sand, hoping things would magically go away. Unfortunately, I carried that over into adult life, which would then, eventually, be the contributing factor to my future downfall.

After weeks of hearing my parents talk about this issue we were having, I distanced myself even more and just locked myself away in my room and played video games. I remember they called me downstairs one day and said, "Ronnie, we have some news, we're moving in the next few weeks". I was distraught! (For about thirty seconds). Then they told me we were moving only 4 miles away to live in a bungalow. Without hesitation, I smiled. I couldn't help it. I could see the relief on my parents' faces. For some reason, I always wanted to live in a bungalow. Which would later be known as the "Jungalow". It might seem weird for a kid just turning fourteen years old to want to live in what was essentially a home for older folks. Then I realised what it was and why it appealed to me so much as a kid. I thought it would be safer if we were all on one floor. I know that makes no sense, but in my young mind, it did at the time, and I had to grasp onto whatever I could back then.

It had now been over a year of sleeping in my mum and dad's room, I had this deep inner fear that I wasn't going to wake up in the mornings. Because I saw my brother go so young, it was like anything was possible. Maybe this could be a good thing. It was a bungalow for disabled people. The discs in my dad's spine were crumbling at a rapid rate. He had been crushed in a machine whilst working in a marble mason factory not long before I was born. Plus, he was still very much battling with the aftermath of the operation. Mum was also classified as not fit for work. They had worked tirelessly all their lives, and I know my dad, in particular, was struggling with the adjustment. He was a real get-up-and-go type of guy. He never took anything from anyone and had the pride of a pack of lions. That refusal to be beaten and 'get up and go' attitude my dad possessed would later go on to be something I ingrained into my life.

In late 1998, the move started to happen; I actually couldn't wait. The only concern of mine was making new friends in a different area. I was still completely vacant at school and was trying to bunk off as much as I could physically get away with. Whether that be blagging sick days off or disappearing during the day while actually at school. When my mum and dad took me to look at the bungalow for the first time, there was a slight glimmer of hope. As soon as I walked in, I felt at home. Even though there were no carpets or wallpaper, I knew it wouldn't be like that forever! I walked around an even smaller playground and felt a degree of contentment I hadn't experienced before. Maybe it was just being completely out of Cobham that did that for me back then. I'm not entirely sure. I know my parents were glad to be out of the village. It was a nice place, but the people were all of a certain ilk, and if you didn't fit the mould, you'd be judged and looked down on for it. I think we were much happier away from the close-nit community and solum memories. It was a fresh start for all of us.

Once we got settled in, I started to go out gradually and explore the area a bit. I started meeting new kids in the village and eventually made a new group of friends. Meopham was a much bigger place in comparison and there was slightly more to do there. I was still friends with Lizzy and Adam at this point; they used to come down and see me sometimes. It was rare for Lizzy, as she lived in Surrey, getting down wasn't as easy anymore. The first two years of living in Meopham were some of my happiest days around that time, without a doubt. I was blissfully unaware of how bad things were regarding my mum. Maybe I was a bit too young to fully recognise the issues. I still spent as much time out of the house as I possibly could.

Mum was hard to be around, and dad was still ill. I didn't know how to process it, so I kept my head down. In the hope that it would go away. Life doesn't work like that, but becoming insular was the only way I had learned to cope. I made a new bunch of friends and loved going out with them all, but my demeanor indoors was a different kettle of fish. At this point, mum and dad stepped in with an intervention. My temper was seriously out of control. I was hitting things in the house, smashing stuff up, fighting at school, and becoming completely unapproachable. It was the only way I could vent. I didn't cry much as a child. I think it just came out in pure rage rather than emotion. I recall vividly that my mum and dad sat me down and said, we've got a lady coming over. She's going to take you out and get you some dinner to get you out of the house. My reply was, "She better not be a counsellor". I was already on to them; they promised me faithfully that she wasn't, it was just to give me a break from home life and nothing else.

I reluctantly went along. This lady was reminiscent of Sue Pollard, the English actress and singer. Her name was Sheila, when she arrived, I noticed her happy and friendly demeanor, but I was extremely cautious. Sheila took me to McDonald's, which was an absolute winner, we were off to a good start. But I was very sceptical. In the back of my mind, I was thinking, why would a woman who I don't know from Adam be taking me out for dinner - unless there was an ulterior motive! We sat down at a table and started eating. Sheila started asking a few questions, nothing too pushy or personal. I was okay with that. I put it down to general chit-chat than anything else. Then she asked something personal, and I immediately thought, ah, here we go. I shelled up a bit hoping she's not going where I think she is with this. Before I knew it, she got these cards out of her purse and splayed them across the table. Each card had a different emotion written on them. She proceeded to ask, "How does that make you feel?". I'm sure I just muttered something vague and unassuming. As soon as I had eaten my Happy Meal, I asked her to take me back. I barely said a word to her the whole way home. I was fucking fuming; I never forgave my parents for lying to me like that. I was so disappointed, I know they were trying to help me, but they lied. It was unforgivable to me. It destroyed my trust in them.

As soon as I stepped foot indoors, I told them not to talk to me again. "You lied; I fucking knew you were tricking me". If anything, it made me ten times worse. Now, I was angry at them when I wasn't necessarily beforehand. I was just lost and didn't know what the fuck was going on in my life. I suppose it was a

44

panic response to help me. They'd already lost one son, and they probably thought that I was going to head down the same road as my brother, but it made matters worse indoors. I had no one I could trust other than my sister and she had her own life with her family.

Things went from bad to worse until we were all on our separate paths of grief. We were all living under the same roof but miles apart. It was a tragically sad situation. The aftermath of David's death had long-lasting effects. Dad developing cancer. Anger seething through me leading to my self-destruction. Mum would sadly fall into developing an unhealthy addiction. A path that unfortunately would never end for her. It would manifest into a long, winding, dark tunnel of torment and trauma that we would all get dragged into, and there was nothing anyone could do to stop it!

Chapter 6

The Domino Effect - Part 2

I started to notice around the age of fifteen, that mum's behaviour was getting strange and more unpredictable. She became vacant and seemed disinterested in anything going on around her. I used to hear her and dad arguing regularly, normally about bills. I heard dad saying, "we don't have the fucking money Meg". It didn't take long for me to start putting the pieces of the puzzle together. Mum was drinking heavily. We were skint at the time; my dad was trying to dissuade her. We all assumed it was her way of dealing with my brother's suicide. It would shockingly become apparent that wasn't the case. We came to find that information out a year after her passing in 2018. One of her best mates told us she was drinking heavily in the 80's. This revelation meant that she hadn't acquired this habit after David had died at all. It came as quite a shock to my sister and I. As that was mum's excuse for many years!

School life was quickly coming to an end. The pressure of exams that I didn't study for were looming over me. I just went in with the hope that I would do okay. My best grade was a distinction in science. The rest were E's and Fs across the board, which wasn't surprising. When I cast my mind back to the last day of school, I recall many kids crying their eyes out. Mostly girls, but some of the boys were also upset. But, for me, I couldn't wait to get out of there. Some of my classmates were discussing the possibility of staying on for Sixth Form. My grades were not even good enough to do that. Not that I had any intention of staying in that shit hole. I walked out of those doors in 2000 and never looked back. With an unwavering air of confidence that what was be outside of those gates would be considerably better! Oh, how wrong I was, if anything, it was worse. I couldn't get into any decent colleges or even begin to think of university. I had complete disregard and arrogance for how the real world worked. I was in for a shock!

After I left Secondary School, I dossed about, as I thought I had all the time in the world. One of my close friends, Ginger Chris would come over regularly. We'd stay up all night playing Sega Bass fishing on the Dreamcast and Snake on our Nokia phones. I didn't understand that his family were financially stable, unlike my own, who were on the breadline. There is one hilarious story that is permanently scorned onto my brain from one night that Chris happened to fall asleep on my sofa. He only lived around the corner, so when he woke up in the early hours of the morning, he walked home to go to his part-time job with his dad. He was confronted by the local psychopathic dog of the village. This dog had cornered him, and he had nowhere to go other than to jump on top of a car. The funny thing was, that I had melted a square of dairy milk chocolate on his forehead while he was asleep, and it was still there when he went home. His dad managed to save him from the dog. When Chris got down from the car roof, his dad quizzed him about what was stuck to his head. I got an angry phone call immediately. I was laughing then and I am laughing now whilst writing this over twenty years later. Just the imagery it creates in my head still tickles me.

When I wasn't knocking about with Ginger Chris, I would be doing some form of dangerous hobby with my friends Phil and Dan. It started with trials riding on our mountain bikes, jumping up and down stupendously high things. A hobby which is largely responsible for the majority of the scars I carry today. Our other passion was skateboarding, which would become my favourite of them all. Phil and I would go to Rochester or Swanley some weekends. Those were some genuinely good times, and it was my first taste of freedom. There was something about it that brought me some peace. When I wasn't bound to my local area, I would infrequently go to Surrey to see Lizzy, to have a welcome break from the tension indoors and catch up with my best pal. That was where I discovered weed. All of her mates were party animals, and my word, did we get shitfaced at every single opportunity. I got along well with all her friends and her boyfriend. There were a couple of weekends in particular that never left my memory. One of which was when we all went to a massive funfair. Some of the lads had some weed, and we all had a few lagers. It was the first time I had properly smoked it, and at the time, I didn't know what I was getting into. If you're new to smoking weed, it's not advisable to start with white widow. If you don't know what that is, it's an extremely potent strain. Especially for a first-timer.

We got to the amusements, and we're all buzzing. I remember getting onto this ride. It was a circular cage you stood up in. A seat belt would go across your torso to keep you locked in. When this ride started to spin, the G-force it generated would push your back into the wall of the ride. As soon as the belt went over my chest, I didn't feel right. Then BOOM! Out of nowhere, I pulled a whitey, and it was too late to get off the ride. It was just about to start. I didn't know what a whitey was at this point. But I found out extremely quickly! Only one minute into the ride, I lost my vision and couldn't see anything other than blurred lights. My knees buckled and gave way, I nearly passed out. My friend next to me was trying to hold me up. When I got off the ride, I threw up and laid on my back with the world just swirling above me. I recall one of the fairground workers coming over to me and asking if I was okay. I replied, "Yeah, cheers, mate, I think I'm fine". He was just a tall, dark silhouette that was talking. I couldn't make out any of his features whatsoever! My friends came back over to me and were laughing, but a little concerned at the same time. They picked me up, and we tentatively walked on. Any other rides were out of the question, and weed was off the menu for the rest of the evening. Little did I know that would be the prerequisite to a decade-long drug problem, resulting in some near-fatal experiences.

I spent a lot of time in Surrey; there was never a dull moment. One night, Lizzy had fallen out with her cousin, who was part of a gang. If my memory serves me correctly, they were called 'LBT.' And no, it didn't stand for lettuce, bacon, and tomato. Not as far as I am aware, anyway. I was walking with Lizzy and her friend Steph late one night; we got a call saying to be on guard.

They're looking for her. Being the only bloke amongst us at that time, I had to stay alert! The other guys from our group were at least twenty minutes away. I knew that potentially it could be a bad night from that moment on. My fight-or-flight response kicked in instantly. I decided, if I was going out, which was highly likely, I was going out fighting! I ripped a fence post out of the ground and just hoped it wouldn't come to it. But if it did, then I'd take my beating, but definitely hurt one of them in the process. We proceeded to walk up the road; it had been ten minutes, and there was no sign of them. Thank God! Then, out of nowhere, a handful of lads walked out behind a bush in front of us from someone's garden. They approached us, and it was Lizzy's cousin, he immediately got in her face. Bearing in mind, he was a boy doing this to a girl. Honestly, it was low-level stuff. I clenched the wooden post in my hand. I already decided it was going around his head if he hit her. She called him a prick and told him to do one. Luckily, nothing came of it. Then, our boys came around the corner only minutes afterwards. I have never been so relieved to see people in my life.

There was always some sort of drama in Surrey, that was a factor as to why Lizzy and I stopped talking eventually. That and the fact that our relationship was a very odd one. All the time I was single, she just wanted to be my mate, and every time I got a girlfriend, she wanted more. I could never work that out. When I arrived home from my stay in Surrey, I reverted to type, and thought if I buried my head in the sand, it'd all work itself out, but it never did. 2002 was rapidly approaching. Even though I had become quite reclusive and distanced myself from the large majority of people that were once close. I knew deep down it was all going to change soon. I spent more time at home, witnessing what was going on around me. I became hyper-aware of the seriousness of my family situation. I couldn't just sit around listening to music and watching TV all day, every day. I wasn't wrong. One morning, my dad opened my bedroom door and said, "You better sort your fucking life out son. You're not living here for free. You have two months to get a job, further your education, or you're out!" I'll never forget that, and it was the boot-up the proverbial I very much needed at the time.

My dad was a grafter, he was brought up in South Bermondsey by a no-nonsense dad and a tough as nails mother who didn't suffer fools gladly. So, there wasn't a cat in hell's chance I was getting away with that carry-on. I reluctantly came to the realisation that I had no choice. I asked my dad for help, as I didn't know where to turn or what I could do for work with my terrible grades. After looking around at my limited options, I ended up going to North West Kent College to do a course in retail and warehousing. I was then allocated a placement via the college to get some work experience (A Charity Shop). It wasn't ideal, I was so embarrassed to work there because of the stigma around them, but I had no choice unless I was to quit. Which wasn't an option as I had only just started. My dad would have gone ape-shit if I walked out in my first week. I didn't want to let him down. He had been through enough!

On my first week working at the new placement. I quickly discovered Glenda, the 'boss', was a horrible, uptight middle-aged woman who didn't want to be there any more than I did. She did her best to make my life harder than it already was. Luckily for me, there was a saving grace her name was Lisa. She was the assistant manager, and was a sweetheart. She was a lot younger and saw things more from my point of view. She would regularly check up on me and make sure I was okay. I think she probably knew I had stuff going on in the background. Despite Glenda being the boss from hell, she may have saved my arm from being amputated. I was only a few months into working there, and I had just had a huge skateboarding accident, getting flung through the air, landing on my elbow and back. My elbow bone was clearly visible. You could see the whiteness of the bone. Glenda asked me one day to show her the injury. I had this slimy brown/green puss seeping through the makeshift bandage I had wrapped around it. Glenda nearly went grey when she saw it and made me leave work to go to the hospital immediately! Luckily, I did, as the nurse said it was infected, and it could have gotten a lot worse if left much longer without treatment. I got constantly hurt as a teenager, and even to this day, I can't help but put myself in the firing line in some capacity. I never learn.

50

After a few months passed, I had settled into my new work-life. Lisa and I started talking more, she became an older sister figure. Glenda was still making my life hell; she just didn't have any people skills at all. One afternoon, it came to blows as I carried some books down the stairs. She shouted at me in front of everyone, I lost it. I slammed the books on the floor and stormed out. As I walked out, I shouted, "I don't need this shit, my mums in the fucking hospital, I'm off!" She walked after me, but I was long gone. The hilarious side to this story is, two weeks later. I started at a new placement. (The charity shop slap bang opposite.) I thought, Oh no. This is going to be like Millwall Vs West Ham all over again. The first day she saw me, it was hysterical. I just smirked and was like, yep. I went there. I know all your dirty secrets that I can divulge directly to the competition.

I was naturally apprehensive about starting a new placement, but, much to my surprise, all the people were lovely. The management, was great and all the volunteers. The floor manager, Clarisse, was a lovely woman as well. Her younger sister, who I 'might' have slept with in the cellar on top of the charity shop bags, was also a 'little treat'. Bless her heart. I was only there for a short period of time, as I had to move on to complete my N.V.Q Level 2. I didn't want to leave when the time came. My college tutor, Raymond, was a top bloke. He always had our best interests at heart and was the most chilled-out guy going. He'd let us play our music on his stereo when we came into the class, as long as we got on with the work. I usually had a Drum and Bass tape on me without fail! Even though I am 100% sure it did his nut in, he still let us crack on. He was a decent guy and a positive role model in my life. I don't think he understood the impact that he had on me as a teenager. I don't think I even realised it myself.

When I started the second phase of my training, I went to work in a warehouse called Espirit. They were based in the village, only a mile away from where I lived. I didn't even know they existed until that point. Although I didn't want to leave my current placement, it was a good opportunity that I couldn't turn down. I was starting to develop even more of a passion for music.

This is when I discovered Hip Hop. It had taken my life by storm. I had listened to many different genres, but this was something different. My whole life changed when I played Illmatic by Nas. It was the first time I could see the imagery of what someone was describing in a song, it blew me away! Hip Hop in many ways became my comfort blanket, whenever I felt I needed to escape I would play an album and forget the world around me.

I remember being nervous in my first week working at Espirit. I was certainly not the confident man I am today. I had a slightly better attitude than the kid that was fresh out of school, and I think my dad was relieved that seemed to be the case. He still had his hands full with mum, and at this point, she was completely off the rails. The alcohol had a vice-like grip over her life now, and that's all she cared about. I was out of the house five days a week, working, and out on the weekends with friends, so I was oblivious how bad things had got and how far she had regressed. Work became a distraction if nothing else.
I settled in quickly at Espirit. Six months later, I had done enough to pass my N.V.Q. level 2. Espirit then offered to take me on full-time. I accepted, despite the money being woeful! It was better than the £50 a week I was previously being paid as a temp. The majority of the staff were good eggs. I would often spend all my lunch breaks playing pool in the social area with Gary. I always enjoyed the game growing up and had a naturally good eye for it.

When Gary and I were on different lunch breaks, I would happily sit down at the computer and spend time researching my newfound love of Hip Hop. In 2002 the internet was painfully slow. I think it may have even been dial-up. So, I had a limited timeframe to consume the knowledge I craved during that hour. The first artists I discovered were Nas, Mos Def, Talib Kweli, Common, and the Wu-Tang Clan. Just to name a few. I didn't know that Hip Hop would forever have such a profound effect on me or that I would later go on to become a writer and an Emcee myself. Music consumes me far more these days, it became apparent that it's a contributing factor as to why I'm still here.

Three months into permanent employment, and it's going well. A new lad starts. I'm no longer the fresh meat of the company, which was nice. He was only sixteen. You could tell he was from a good background. He was well-spoken, all his clothes were designer, and he was clearly an intelligent boy. He adapted well to the working environment. I spent two weeks training him, whilst also taking on a few other responsibilities in different departments. Things were running quite smoothly, until I got called into the office only weeks later. I thought it might be some praise for my hard work. As soon as I walked through the door, I knew that wasn't going to be the case, as three of them were sitting there all looking very serious. Two directors, the floor manager and Derek, the 'boss'. He had a huge stack of picking notes in his hand, he put them on the table and said, "can you explain these?". I was so confused and didn't know what he was talking about. I replied; "I'm not sure what you're asking me?". Derek leaned forward in his chair with a serious demeanor, "All of those items you see before you on these picking notes are missing". It then dawned on me what they were accusing me of. "Wait, do you think I am responsible for these missing items, you think I have stolen them?". Derek didn't hesitate or lose face "we believe it to be you, and after some investigation, it seems you're the only person it could be". What he meant to say was you're a little rude boy; you look capable of doing it; therefore, we're blaming you, and that's it!

They sacked me on the spot, I was then unfairly and abruptly escorted out of the building. A completely innocent man who had not stolen anything from the warehouse, ever! I'd been there for a year at this point. Why would I start stealing now? I was in a state of shock, upset, confused and completely and utterly dejected. I walked home in disbelief, thinking, how on earth will I fucking explain this to my parents? Will they even believe me? In my head, I was fuming, and I thought to myself, Can I get a break!?!?! I have worked so hard in college just to get to this point. My mum and dad were finally off my back and somewhat "proud" of me. Now I had to go home and tell them I am back in the same position I was just over two years ago when Dad walked into my room and told me to sort my fucking life out and get a job.

I trepidatiously started walking home to confront my parent's and tell them what had just happened. I opened the door and sheepishly gave them the bad news. My old man said, "Well, did you do it?". I can't blame him, his first son as you've all learned was a thieving git. So, his scepticism was understandable in the circumstances. I replied, "of course I didn't. I swear, I promise you! But I've still lost my job for something I never did". I was at a low point. I didn't have a clue where to turn next. My dad was quite abrupt and said, "well, don't dwell on it. Go and get another job. You have the experience and qualifications now". A week goes by, and I still can't believe what has happened. I remember sitting in my room thinking, how can I prove my innocence?

Two more weeks pass, I'm talking to a friend outside my house when my phone rings. It's a mobile number I don't recognise. I answered it, in case it was important. The voice on the other end says, "Ronnie?". I replied, "Yep, who is speaking?". The man's voice replied, "It's Derek from Espirit!" I felt myself jolt back a bit but was curious as to what he had to say. In a less than welcoming manner I said, "Oh, hello". Then he said "I had called you to say we've made a mistake. We owe you a huge apology, and we would also like to offer you your job back if you want to accept it, of course". I stayed silent as he continued, "We caught the thief red-handed yesterday, and the police are dealing with the matter. I can't tell you how sorry we all are, Ronnie". Remember the clean-cut rich kid from the well-off family? Need I say more. As the old saying goes, don't judge a book by its cover. I told Derek that I'd need to think about it, and that I'd call him in due course. I wanted my dad's advice on the matter before making any snapshot decisions. That was the first time I showed some form of decorum and adult mindset. My dad's instant response was beggars can't be choosers, and it wasn't the time to let ego and pride get in the way. I think he was just a bit afraid that we were in trouble financially as a family and he needed me to contribute, which I don't blame him. I rang Derek later that day and told him I'd take the job back, albeit reluctantly. If I remember rightly, I think I got a little pay raise to ease the blow. When I went back, everyone couldn't believe what they had done and that I had brushed it off. I wouldn't have entertained that offer today. Purely because I don't put up with being treated in such a way. It was an early lesson in doing what was right for the overall situation of everyone involved, especially for my dad. I mean, I didn't do that much for him in hindsight.

It wasn't long after I accepted my old job back when I met Rhian. I got a phone call one night from Adam asking me to come out and meet some girls. Rhian and I didn't exactly hit it off. For some reason we instantly clashed and were goading one another and winding each other up. To the point where the people around us were saying, What's wrong with you two? After a month of frequently spending time with the new group and Rhian. Something seemed to change. We ended up falling for each other, much to people's disbelief! That initial dislike was obviously misread by us both. Because twelve years later, we were still together.

Finally, life was looking a little rosier compared to a few months prior. I had settled back in at work; Rhian and I were still on our honeymoon period. It was nice to have some positivity for a change. I had just been given a promotion at work. Well, more of a sidestep with a better label, as someone had just left. That meant there was a job available. A week later, a distinctive looking bloke turns up for an interview. I thought he was a goth at first. I saw his long black hair from a distance, when I got closer, I noticed that he had dreadlocks. I was quietly curious about this bloke and wondered if he would get the job. Three days go by, before I know it, he's started work on my floor. I went over to introduce myself and say hello. His name was Rick, he had a grin like a Cheshire cat and a noticeable energy about him. We hit it off instantly! One of the first things out of his mouth was, "Do you smoke weed?". I was like, "yeah, I do, mate", and that was it! After a couple of days of getting to know each other, we went down to the pub in our lunch break, getting high as the clouds. A shit version of Cheech & Chong. We only had a beer each, but that wasn't the problem. It was the fact that we started mixing 'Squidgy Black' and 'Skunk' in the same joints. We'd go back to work and float through the door. I was ultra-paranoid, and he didn't give a shit. The wanker would always do something outlandish and stupid to make me laugh just before walking in. Normally, a dance that was called whoop leg. A ludicrous one-legged dance. We went back one day, and he does it. Right outside the door, then nonchalantly walks in as if nothing had happened. I had to take a swift turn down one of the isles to wipe the tears of laughter off my face. I was in such a state, it was unreal! How we didn't get the sack, I'll honestly never know. It was good to have a partner in crime at work and have a laugh.

Unfortunately, this brief period of reprieve for me was short-lived. Although my relationship was still going well, and I'd made a new mate. The weed habit was becoming an issue. I kept it from my parents for quite some time. Especially my sister, after what my brother had already put them all through with his drug addiction. I didn't want them to panic. It was only a bit of harmless weed, after all. Well, that's what I thought. When I initially began smoking it at the age of eighteen, an eighth would last me a week, and I'd be stoned off one joint. By the time 2004 rolled around, barely a year later. That had tripled, easily! I was smoking skunk almost exclusively. My mood swings were bad when I couldn't get any, which was quite rare; nevertheless, it wasn't a good thing. Everyone around me would inevitably pay the price. Again, it was another form of escapism for me. If I was high, I wouldn't have to contemplate reality. I could just smile and worry about stuff the next day, week, month, or year. Ultimately, this was the start of the avalanche!

I was quickly becoming the most selfish person I had ever known, but I couldn't see the wood for the trees at the time. Much to the detriment of everybody else, "getting on it" would be my only goal in life. Yes, I was young lad. I can sit here now and wish I'd done things differently; it's all said and done now, so what's the point in agonising over it? Rick and I were now getting stoned every single day at work, and I was getting lazier and lazier as time went on. I couldn't function like he could whilst high. He'd zone in, and I'd zone out. Which would later cost me my job at Espirit. I would go and do the only other thing I knew. Retail.

Around then, I had become best friends with Rick. He introduced me to some of his mates; Ash, Manny, his sister Cindy, and her then-boyfriend Marky G. We would hook up regularly and party into the small hours of the morning, without a care in the world. Rhian would join in with proceedings as she got on with them all as well. Although she never touched drugs. Rhian said vehemently to me one day that she wouldn't put up with me doing anything else like cocaine or pills. I didn't blame her to be honest, but that never occurred to me at that time. I'd then meet Rick's other friends, Mo and Jason. We started going to music gigs all over the U.K. Mainly dub/reggae nights. I was on a slippery slope, but I didn't realise it at the time. I was just having fun with my friends and partying. I was only doing what most young guys did at that age. What could go wrong?

Chapter 7

New Start - Old Habits

After being laid off by Espirit for my lack of effort and wayward behaviour, to put it mildly. I had to get back into work, I couldn't afford to sit around like I did in previous years. Luckily, my dad knew the manager of a local shop, that was not far from where we lived. He had an opening for an assistant manager position. I didn't want it, I preferred not to work in retail. Terrible money, shocking hours, and having to be nice to the ungrateful, self-entitled people who flooded the shop day in and day out, wasn't my idea of fun. But I had to do something. I still didn't drive, and that was a massive handicap, as it restricted me to the local areas. I took the job purely to keep the peace at home. Things were gradually getting worse and worse; mum was coming home pissed out of her face in the middle of the afternoon. Even my parent's friends had decided to distance themselves. To make matters worse, the neighbours were picking up on it as well. Unfortunately, my mother would bring shame on our family. She started to ask others to buy her alcohol, began thumbing lifts up and down the village, or into the local town centre. She even brought my friends into it, I was so embarrassed, and she didn't care or even begin to consider any of us.

One particular day mum came home so drunk that I just lost it. When she fell through the door, I said, give me your bottle of drink. I was sharply told to fuck off. I was sitting on the front step fixing my bike at the time. I got up and said, "where is it"? I tried grabbing her handbag off her, as she turned away, I went to yank it off her shoulder. I didn't realise it was around her neck. I nearly pulled her head off! I was so enraged; I just couldn't cope with it anymore. I did apologise, even whilst encapsulated in a red mist. I took the vodka out of her bag and hid it in my bedroom. She came in and said, "You better give me that back in a second or I am telling your dad what you've done". I ignored her request, shut my door and carried on mixing Drum & Bass on my turntables. She walked back in ten minutes later, tapped me on the shoulder, and said, "Give me my fucking bottle of vodka back". I said no and turned my back on her. I was just being cruel to be kind. I got a huge clump around the back of my head, it felt like I'd been with a blunt instrument. My mum wore rings on every finger. I ripped my headphones off, threw them down, and turned around to see her standing there, grimacing at me. I noticed something running down the back of my head. I touched my crown, then looked at my hand; there was blood pouring out of my head. I snapped! I picked her up with one arm, walked her out of my room, put her back on her feet outside the door. Looked at my dad and said, "Get her the fuck away from me right now!" I remember as soon as I shut the door, I nearly put my fist through my cupboard in complete rage. I can't even remember if I gave the bottle of vodka back in the end. I think I did. Mainly so my dad could have a quiet life, by this point that was all he needed.

Although dad had bounced back from the cancer, he still had loads of aches and pains and was never the same since. He spent most of his time in the garden tinkering about with his plants. That was 'his' escape when he couldn't go out with his friends. These were some of the worst years for our family, since my brother's death. So much had happened, and there was far too much water under the bridge to turn back now. My dad and I got along, but clashed sometimes because of our similar personalities. I couldn't bear to be anywhere near my mum though. I understood she had lost her son, and it's different for a mother, as they gave birth to the child. But she single-handedly tore our family down further and refused any help. It was like I didn't matter at all. I thought maybe because you'd lost one son, you'd do your best for the other. Not that it was her fault, of course, what happened to David. It was none of our fault. Although I would later go on to get the blame.

It was nigh on impossible to focus on anything, when so much was going on in the background. First week of my unwanted new job. My dad's mate got sacked within three days of me being there, as the store got robbed. After 18 years of loyal service. Some teenagers went around the front of the shop to distract him, whilst the others went around the back to steal a recently delivered batch of cigarettes. The area manager said it was his fault and sacked him for being negligent and not locking them away while he served the other customers. I worked with a temporary manager for nearly six months, while trying to learn the ropes. The situation was less than favourable, but I got on with it and tried the best I could. The money was worse than what I was on before, and I was doing over 80 hours a week some weeks. It was driving me into the ground, but I put up with it and carried on for the sake of helping out indoors. Unfortunately, I wasn't the same lad that I used to be. The weed had taken hold of me; I wouldn't say boo to a goose. I rarely answered anyone back unless I was forced to, and things were so bad indoors that I tried to avoid any confrontation outside of home. I just wanted a quiet life. Then Mr. Brown started. The only way I can describe this guy is the stereotypical bullied school kid, out for his revenge. He did his best to be an arsehole and rub people up the wrong way. He nearly got filled in a few times, once by a local person and again by some Irish travellers after he shouted at their kids. Which I was willing to happen. I wouldn't have helped him at all. I'd love to run into that guy these days. Not that I'd do anything to him, just look him dead in the eye and see him squirm. I am far from that skinny weed smoker now.

Despite my wanting to iron him out, I thought I'd be cleverer than that. The wages were barely covering my bills and weed habit, so I got a bit light-fingered during my shifts alone. I was being treated like crap by the company, the boss, and all the customers. It was time to get something for me now. I would have an extra three hundred pounds a month in my pocket until I finally left. I won't say how I did here; I don't want to give people ideas. It's possibly a viable option even today. I was a lot smarter than people gave me credit for. Mr. Brown was going to find out the hard way. That I was his worst nightmare, and he would fail to catch on quickly enough. He set loads of sneaky traps, but I saw them all from a mile off. When I used to come in the next day after not biting on any of his traps, he gave me this look. I'm on to you, but I don't know how to catch you. He'd messed with the wrong person. Straight away, I want to say this wasn't anything to be proud of, and I'm not bragging, but things nearly went a lot further. There was a post office attached to the shop. A few people in my immediate circle at the time were asking about it, whether it was a viable option to rob. I wasn't keen on the idea to be honest. The plan was; I'd get a knock at the back door from 'the robbers', take a few slaps for authenticity and they'd make off with the cash. It wasn't possible, and even if it was, I wouldn't have gone through with it. Even back then I had some limits!

I have painted myself as quite an awful person thus far, haven't I? But I will treat anyone, and I mean anyone with respect if they're decent people. I'd die for my close friends and any of the people I love without even blinking. But if you cross me, especially for no reason, then you reap what you sow. Eye for an eye, tooth for a tooth. It may sound a bit nasty, but many people feel the same and just wouldn't say it. I would like to think most people would speak decently of me these days. I'm far from perfect, but I'm also far from the guy that I used to be. I will give anyone time and help them if it's in my power. Mr. Brown on the other hand, didn't realise the gravitas of his mistake until I was already out the door. I shall tell you how I got him back. Bearing in mind that his job was to 'save' the shop. I took what was in my eyes, rightfully owed to me. After working an extra 20 hours a week out of my contract. In my last week, I pulled out all the stops.

A rep from high up in the company came into our store to review the itinerary and layout of the cards. She went ballistic that the whole floor plan for the cards were back to front. Mr. Brown wasn't at work that day. The lady said "I'm not having a pop at you, my love. This is all his fault". She spent three hours there angrily swapping it around and said she'd be back in two weeks to check up on it. She asked me to pass the message on to him when he got back. Which I happily did. I knew I wouldn't be there when she came back. Well, I think we can see where this is going. As soon as she walked out the door, I spent two hours putting it all back. Not only that, I sabotaged it further by mixing every different genre of card. while I was there, I thought it'd be rude to leave the magazines out. So, I spent another hour doing those as well. I wish I could have been a fly on the wall when she turned up two weeks later. I didn't stop there though. It was at the height of summer. The shop had no air conditioning, and we were sweltering every day. A massive ice cream delivery arrived, which happened to be worth over £700. It went in the big chest freezer out the back. We already had around £400 worth in there. Friday night was the handover of the keys. I had a new job at a well-known Supermarket stacking shelves. I know. What a high flyer! I was contemplating what else I could do before leaving. I walked past the freezer and thought to myself, I'll take the plug out! Nope, that is far too obvious I said to myself. But it's a great idea, the execution just needs to be better. So, I left it plugged in. I just gently wiggled the plug out of the socket until I heard it go from a noticeable whirring sound to dead silence. Mr. Brown arrives at 5:45pm to do the handover. We walk out together at 6:15pm. He locks the door. It was over thirty degrees in that shop, even at night. The chocolate had to be removed from the shop floor, as it was running off the shelves. It got stored out the back, and even that wasn't working, melting every day and getting thrown out in most cases! I dread to think what that £1000 plus worth of ice cream looked like 14 hours later. I mean, I'm far from an expert, but it was probably of a runny disposition.

I found out a couple of months later, Mr. Brown had stormed out. With the ice cream having to be written off. The rep from the card company returned as promised two weeks later, who inevitably must have drop-kicked him after all the hard work she'd done. Plus doing all those long hours. It probably took its toll, bless him. I do feel a bit guilty now. Oh, wait! Nope! No, I Don't. He had no respect for me, was rude to my mum on the phone, treated everyone like dirt, and had an issue with women in general. He just spread negativity wherever he trod. So, he got what was coming to him. Manners and respect don't cost anything until they do. I know the whole story is petty and childish, but sometimes there's room for it when you are in your early twenties. I walked out of there with a big grin and left him perplexed.

I thought working in a Supermarket would be a doddle to be honest. But they bunged me in the frozen section. It was like working in Antarctica. The hours were probably some of the worst I had ever done, the shifts were either 10 am to 6pm or 2 pm to 10 pm. I used to 'wake and bake' before going in for my early shift, just to handle it. It had that corny team feeling. I hate that sort of stuff. There was a thing that used to happen around lunchtime called 'rumble time'! Everyone would stop what they were doing and run to the nearest shelf to tidy it up and put everything in order. They were so enthusiastic, that it made me throw up in my mouth. But as usual, I kept my head down and went about my day as quietly as possible. The assistant manager was out the front one day, I walked in as what I can only describe as ferociously high. My eyes were like piss holes in the snow. I was as white as a ghost and looked like I hadn't slept for the last decade. Nothing tells you how stoned you are until you turn up for work and walk into the most brightly lit area on earth, faced with hundreds of people and a suspicious boss. Her first words were, "What's wrong with your eyes today, Ronnie?" I thought on my feet and straight away said, "ah, I have bad hay fever." She said, "oh dear, go down aisle eight, there's some antihistamines there". I luckily got away with it that time. I don't think she was overly convinced.

This moment in my life was a very murky and self-destructive period for me. I didn't have much care for anything going on. I just lived in a bubble of negativity and refused to climb out of it. I'd go to work just because I had to. I had zero interest in it, and that would become apparent when I quit working there within about two months. I just couldn't handle the environment at all. It was overwhelming for me. I felt like I was constantly being watched. Whether that was the paranoia from smoking pot or they were actually watching me, I'm not sure. But it was likely a combination of the two. What with the drugs and drinking too much; I was just slowly spiraling out of control and didn't have the foresight at the time to rectify my predicament. But then, if

63

you don't know that there is a problem, how are you supposed to address it? I realise now, how much of a dark place I was in. I couldn't hold a job down for much longer than a year, 18 months at the most. With no aspirations or direction, I decided to sign up to an agency. The agency signed me up to work on a building site, doing hard labour. That was reasonably short-lived as well. My main objective in life between 2006 - 2008 was to smoke weed and escape reality! When reflecting on this, I can't believe what a loser I was—just a pointless human being, digging himself a deeper hole to crawl into.

In amongst all this madness, dad's cancer had come back with a vengeance. In June 2008 he was told by the doctor, that he had three to six months to live. Although all of us were expecting him to pass on any day, it's still hard to process and deal with. We start talking about plans for his funeral, what to do, and if we could have all his old friends' numbers, to contact them. It was very depressing, but the sad reality of life. When discussions initially started, dad, in his infinite wisdom, had an idea. Dad turned to us and said, "What's the point in all my old friends being there when I'm fucking dead?" So, my sister Tracey said "Let's have your wake now Dad, so you can be there to enjoy it!" And that's exactly what happened. It made the local paper and later the magazine 'Best'. The wake was incredible, the atmosphere was one of a kind. All his friends thought it was an excellent idea, and I'm sure that most of you reading this find it at least slightly humorous. That was my old man all over. He even sang with all the students my sister supported at Mid Kent college. They put on a spectacular show for Ron! I suppose the one good thing about knowing you're dying, is that you can go out with a bang, and that's what he did. Smiling, drinking, and partying to the end. Well, sort of. There was just one problem! He went on to live for another two years. His friends were all saying, "are you going to fucking die or what?" I have to love the humour around a morbid situation; the fight my dad possessed was nothing short of admirable. What a man!

It was a tough time for all of us, none more so than my dad. I knew I couldn't keep burying my head in weed and pretending it wasn't happening. Things desperately needed to change; I couldn't go on the way I was. Plus, I was invited to go on holiday to America and desperately needed the break. Rhian was adamant about going with her sister and her boyfriend. So, it was an opportunity for me to make an effort for once, and put my money into something worthwhile, rather than pissing it up the wall and smoking it. They were all very concerned about me smoking weed out there or getting caught with stuff on me. About six months before we went out to Florida, I quit anyway, much to the surprise and delight of everyone involved. I had loads of spare money due to still living at home and not smoking that crap! I was paying off the holiday in rapid fashion. Most people would think it was due to having a holiday booked, which was the catalyst for me getting clean. But, in all honesty, it wasn't. As cliche as it sounds, I woke up one morning and had an epiphany moment. I always used to stash my stuff in a speaker near my television. The first thing I would do in the morning was wake up, check how much I had left, and see if I needed to make a call to go out later on that evening and get some more. A sad existence when you think about it. I woke up this particular morning and grabbed the bag. I had loads left. I walked to the kitchen bin and threw it away! I had friends I could have given it to. But I wanted it gone there and then. So that's what happened. That was around the early part of 2008. The last drag I ever had on a joint was New Year's Eve that year. I had 4 or 5 puffs to see 2009 in and haven't smoked it since and I never will!

It was scary how much weed took away from me as a person. I could be sitting in a room filled with my best friends yet feel a million miles away. I'd be so uncomfortable, that I wouldn't want to converse with anyone. I was in a constant state of unyielding paranoia, and hyper-conscious of myself. I thought it was just me, and that's who I had become. I didn't want to consider the fact that it could have been the weed, that was the source of all my problems. Well, most of them anyway. I was a shell of my former self; I thought I would go straight back to the man I once was after giving up weed. Unfortunately, that would not be the case. I'll never forget the cold turkey phase. Some may laugh and think it was only a bit of weed; it has different effects on different people. It had a massive life-altering effect on myself. When I was at my worst, I'd be forever accusing people of stuff they never did. Or letting my imagination run so wild that I'd almost create a different reality of life. I was a prisoner in the aftermath of going clean. A descending black hole of torture and misery gripped me and wouldn't let me go. The nightmares, cold sweats, heightened paranoia, and feeling sick were so bad, I didn't know what to do. Luckily, I stuck it out and forced myself to go through what I had to. I had no idea that it would take me the best part of three years to feel around 80% of what I used to be. The first year was nothing short of torture. The nightmares and sweats went on for at least six months. I thought it would never end. The paranoia was actually worse for nearly a year too. Most people would have gone to the doctor and sought some help. In hindsight, that's what I should have done. But it was a battle I was determined to win alone. It wasn't just torture for me. It was torture for everyone around me. I was unbearable to be around 90% of the time. My anger was out of control, and I was in a depressive state of mind that I couldn't seem to shake.

The holiday to Florida was a welcome break. By the time it came around, I was feeling slightly better, but still not myself. Rhian and I were nervous about the flight. It was her first flight ever and it was my first flight since that horrific experience I had coming back from Cyprus ten years prior. When we boarded the plane, both overcome by nerves and fear. I was thinking two things. What are the chances of something going wrong with my second flight in a decade? And the other being. Well, my luck isn't exactly great is it. I was in a constant fight with myself the whole time. Three hours into the journey, we hit a pocket of turbulence. The pilot announced that it may be a rocky ride for a while and to not worry, just stay seated. Ten minutes go by, and we are in the most horrific situation, which feels like a near death experience. The plane was eerily silent. Everyone clutched, with desperation, onto their seats for dear life. Then, out of nowhere, the plane plummeted over a thousand feet and dropped out of the sky. The only reason I know this, is because on long-distance flights they have a LCD screen with a map on the back of the seat in front of you. The information of the altitude of the plane and various other flight details are displayed for your reference. We went from 36,000 feet to just under 35,000 in seconds. I thought that was it. I honestly thought we were all dead. The plane was shaking so violently that the lights were flickering on and off. Even the flight attendants looked visibly perturbed. They strapped themselves in and shut the curtain. Not, something at the time that filled me with confidence. I can honestly say that was probably the most scared I have ever been in my entire life. After what seemed an eternity, in reality, it was probably about 10 minutes. The turbulence passed, everyone let out a massive sigh of relief. No one barely spoke the rest of the flight. We weren't even halfway through the journey. I was up and down to the toilet constantly. I tried to get drunk to take my mind off of what had just happened. Even that wasn't working. I just felt sicker and worse than I did beforehand. When we landed, Rhian's sister Julia and her boyfriend Asher said it was the worst flight they had been on in 16 years. What are the chances? Well, I was still cursed with bad luck when it came to flying. The relief I felt once I had stepped off that plane was immense!

Finally, my feet touched American soil in Florida; it was scorching hot on the verge of 90°F. That sense of relief didn't last long. As the immediate realisation hit me that we still had to fly home. I parked that emotion up and thought, I'll deal with that in two weeks when I have to. The holiday was very much an action-packed one. It involved multiple excursions and theme parks. I was never really a fan of big roller coasters or freefall rides when I was a child. I did warn Asher that I might not be the most fun partner in crime as far as that was concerned. He didn't have to rely solely on me though. Which did take the pressure off. Another couple came along with us, one of Asher's best friends - Big Rich, his wife and son joined the party. He was very excited about being able to go on all the rides. He was a massive guy, 23 stone plus. Over in the UK he was too big to get on the rides, so he was adamant that this was his chance. Busch Gardens was the first park we visited. The first ride we approached was massive. One of the most daring roller coasters to ride in Florida at the time, called 'Montu'. I looked up at it and went, nope! Then I thought to myself. I've just managed a 10-hour flight at 36,000 feet and that fell 1,000 feet out of the sky. I'm sure this isn't 1,000 feet high. With that in mind, I joined the queue. Asher did say to me before we got out there, that if you join a queue, you can't make the chicken walk out of it. It's humiliating! You either grow a pair and go for it or don't bother at all. Well, I was in it now and not turning back. The closer we got, the more my heart pounded and beads of sweat formed on my forehead. Big Rich, Asher's mate wasn't coming on. He said he was going to do it the next day instead. As soon as I sat in that seat, my heart started pounding out of my chest. Asher looked at me and said, "if you can do this one, you'll get on any ride out here. Let's fucking go!!!" I have to admit that his enthusiasm helped me.

We start the slow, ambling climb to the inevitable massive drop that lay before us. We craned slowly over the lip of the drop, then plummeted into a vertical abyss. My heart was in my mouth, and my adrenaline was through the roof. Then, I realised I was loving it. After the second corkscrew and the loop, I was smiling from ear to ear. When we got off, I was buzzing, and wanted to get straight back in the queue for a second go. Big Rich was the only one who didn't look very pleased by my recently newfound love for roller coasters. Everyone else was laughing. Asher was happy as he had a nutter to go on rides with throughout the holiday. I ended up going on every single big ride out there. Despite Big Rich's brave statements in the UK, he never set foot on one ride in the entirety of the two weeks we were there. Florida was certainly an incredible experience and one I will never forget. The two weeks flew by. Then it was time to face the scariest ride of all. my nemesis, flying! Luckily, the flight home was a lot better and unbelievably, I was so exhausted from the holiday that I passed out for over 4 hours on the way home. When I woke up, I was elated to learn that there were only four and a half hours left until we were back in our homeland. As far as I am aware, there wasn't even a pocket of turbulence on the journey back. When we arrived in the UK, I was so tired and jet-lagged. We all had work on Monday morning, which was only three days away. Plus, they had lost my suitcase with all my newly bought clothes in from the States. I wasn't happy in the slightest. Thankfully, it was located and returned to me the next day. I recovered all my goods. Something had to go wrong didn't it... ha-ha!

Whilst I was away, I asked a few close friends to look in on my dad. His cancer was the worst it had been for six years, and he was in a bad way. I remember saying to him before I went on holiday that I wouldn't go to America, and I nearly cancelled at the last minute. My dad was not having it, he refused to let me stay at home. He promised me he would be fine, and I was to go on that holiday. The good mates I trusted to carry out my request and check in on my dad were Phil, Dan, and Spud. All of them were top drawer, honoured their promises, and looked in on my dad while I was away. Which I was extremely grateful for. However, it came to light that one of them exploited the situation for their own benefit.

A week or so after I got back, I walked into the front room, where my dad was slowly withering away, in tremendous pain. He turned around and said to me, "Son. I have got something to tell you, but you have to promise you won't fly off the handle and go around there." As soon as he said the sentence, my back was up. My first thought was, who has done something to my old man while I was away?!?! He looked at me with this apprehensiveness that I rarely saw in my dad's eyes. One of the days Spud popped around to see my dad. At the time, the cancer had gotten so bad that he couldn't even walk. He had to use a wheelchair. He politely asked Spud if he could give him a lift down to the pub that Sunday. The pub in question was only 300 metres away at most! But when you're riddled with bowel cancer and have trouble even standing up, that's a hell of a long way. Spud did take my dad to the pub that day, and my dad said to him when they got there, "Come in. I'll buy you a pint for taking me". Spud replied, "Don't worry about it Ron, I have to go and meet my girlfriend soon". Most people would have left it at that and thought no more about it. The next day, Spud turned up at my house and approached my dad in the front room, where he was sitting. He had some of his pension money laid out on the table, equating to probably about £8. Spud then, as bold as brass. Said, "Ron, can I take a few quid for that lift I gave you yesterday? I

69

need to buy fags". My dad was quite taken aback by this, but said yes anyway. Spud then proceeded to take that £3 off my dying dad and leave with his head held high to go the shop and buy his fags. Obviously, my dad's previous request of not flying off the handle got quickly dismissed. I stormed around his house, banging his door down that afternoon. I knew he was in, and his family, or at least his dad, was in. None of them came to the door. I wasn't surprised at all. None of them had a spine between them. It was from that day that I no longer spoke to Spud. That was over 14 years ago. I wasn't at all bothered by losing another 'friend'. People come and go in life all the time. But ironically, I met two great guys through Spud. Scott and Jon, with whom I am still friends today, Everything and everyone for a reason.

Chapter 8

Divine Intervention

My anger was at an all-time high and dad's health was rapidly going downhill. There was to be a silver lining though; Millwall had made the play-off semi-final. We were going to Wembley to face Scunthorpe. My dad shouldn't have been alive to witness it, but he was blessed and adamant that he was going. I had to get him there to watch it. So, Cindy, Rick's sister, borrowed Rick's shogun, and we all went up there to cheer on the mighty wall. At that time, Rick and I weren't talking, so for him to remove his ego from the situation and still allow us to use his motor was a decent thing to have done. He did it for my old man, and I'll never forget that. The respect my dad got from my friends was unparalleled and rightly so. Maybe that's what brought Rick and I back together again. Cindy went well out of her way to make it all possible. When people come together for someone, beauty in humanity is born. So, I'm eternally grateful to everyone who played their part. Especially Cindy, to make it possible for my dad. I know he was extremely thankful. It's one of those gestures that weighs heavily on the heart.

Marky G, my dad, myself, and a couple of others were dropped right outside. It was as close as we could get, because dad still couldn't walk very far at this point. The painkillers he had been prescribed, allowed him one last big day out. We turned up and the place was packed solid. Millwall fans were everywhere, in their thousands! The atmosphere was electric. I remember having goosebumps when the first whistle went. I have never seen so many Millwall fans in my life, the whole place was enveloped in a wall of sound the whole first half. It's still, to this present day, the most fans of any team that has attended Wembley, and in my humble opinion, Mr. Gary Alexander is still responsible for the greatest goal ever scored there. It was a tremendous shot from a good 35 yards out. Unfortunately, it wasn't enough to win the game, but my old man had a good day out regardless. I don't think he was even that upset that we lost. It was more to get out of the house and have something to look forward to for a change. We dejectedly made our way out of the ground. I and the rest of the lads were gutted about losing. Final score (3-2): We decided to drown our sorrows at the local boozer nearer to home.

It was only a momentary hiatus for my dad, from the negative conditions that awaited him indoors. I felt for the old man; I really did. Because no matter where he went, he couldn't get much peace or be free from pain. If he stayed in, he had my mum to deal with, and if he went out anywhere for too long, he'd be in absolute agony. To add to his agony, the more time went on, the worse mum's alcohol problem got. It was now a popular talking point for the Neighbour's. She was starting to do anything she could to get her hands on drink; it was tearing the family apart even further. My reactions to mums' actions were not helping. There was constant conflict in the home. The arguing was not helping my dad in the slightest, something had to change, and I needed another outlet, other than music.

I hadn't long gotten back from America. One of my best pals, Scott, and his girlfriend Danielle had just started kickboxing and said I should come along. Despite always being fascinated by martial arts as a kid, I was slightly apprehensive at first. I didn't know whether it would be something I'd enjoy. After a few persuasive conversations, I decided to give it a go. I thought, what have I got to lose? I saw it as the perfect excuse to distance myself from the family home. I remember the first time I went; Scott's dad took us all; I was very nervous as I didn't know what to expect. When I walked through the door for the first time, I was met with a class of around 20 people. Some of these guys were very good. I stood in awe of them doing jump-spinning kicks and these fancy moves I had only previously seen in films. Then there was me, a skinny 58kg soaking wet smoker, thinking, yeah, I am out of my league here. The warm-up nearly wrote me off, as my smoker's lungs couldn't handle it at all. I was only 25 years old, but I had already been smoking for 14 years and was in no fit state for such intense cardiovascular activity. But that did not deter me one bit. I came away from there absolutely buzzing from head to toe. I couldn't wait to go again, and that's exactly what I did. Scott was happy I enjoyed it as he had someone else to go with.

Four months go by, and there's a grading for a belt. It's unconventional to have a grading system in Kickboxing, and some people frowned upon it. Although, many of you will understand later, that this grading system wasn't one to be sniffed at, in any way, shape, or form. I was unsure whether I would want to grade. Scott and Danielle talked me into it, and before I knew it, I was at grading evening for my first belt. I am not going to lie; I was shitting myself. I got completely overwhelmed with nerves, desperately trying to recall the moves for the kata I had to perform in front of everyone. You never knew when your name would get called out, so you had to stay fully switched on. Otherwise, you'd get found out. So, unfortunately, there was not one moment to relax. As soon as my name got called, I filled up with anxiety. I just wanted to get through it, but I was also a perfectionist and wanted to do the absolute best I could. There were also a couple of rounds of sparring to get through afterwards. I wasn't sure what to worry about more! Luckily, I passed my first grade with flying colours (phew!) I thought now I'd done it once; the rest of the gradings would be easier. But I'm certain they just got worse as they went along. Each one becomes longer and, notably, a lot harder than the one prior.

Kickboxing did wonders for my anger management, as nothing before had come remotely close to calming me down. So, everyone around me was happy and reaping the benefits of that. Although I was still suffering a lot from the after-effects of smoking weed, and my paranoia and temper were still ever present. It took the edge off. After a few months had passed, I am slowly but surely getting to grips with the more technical side of the sport. The instructor, Ross, approaches me and hints that I am eligible to do a double grading. That meant doing two belts in the same evening. Even though that sounds like it's easier, in the long run, it's not really. Because you still must be extremely proficient in all the moves before you can go on. It just means that on grading night, you have more to do. Ross showed a lot of faith in me, and I didn't want to let him, or myself down. So, the pressure was on, and the grading included the first intermediate belt (Orange). There were some spinning kicks and there were some very technical moves in this belt to master. I wanted to nail them all to show I had been practicing diligently away from the club as well as in lessons.

I was working in a shop at the time. I remember practicing daily, probably hourly if the truth be told. I was obsessed! I started to go through techniques out the back of the shop when it was quiet. I would put something on a shelf to aim at, for my spinning hook kicks. I remember one Sunday afternoon; I was working on my own. Aiming for something on top of a box of Smirnoff Ice, that I used as a target - the idea was to be able to throw the move, but with a degree of control and balance. It seemed logical, that having something to aim for was a good idea. That was until I smashed the box off of the shelf. There was broken glass everywhere! It didn't deter me though. I kept practicing every waking minute I could. If I wasn't physically going through the syllabus, I would be thinking about kickboxing. I didn't want to fail the first meaningful belt. This was the first time in my life I realised I am a hyper-obsessive person when I have a goal in mind. I would have been devastated if I hadn't passed. So, the only option was to practice at every opportunity.

The next grading was fast approaching, and Kickboxing became the focal point of my life. It was nice to channel my energy towards something positive for a change. When grading night arrived, I was overwhelmed with anxiety and the fear of failing. I had practiced the kata a hundred times over, yet I was still worried I would forget everything I learned when it mattered on the night. We got there early, and the worst thing of all, Jason, Ross' instructor, was down from Sheffield with all his kickboxers. When he walked in, the room fell into silence. His students were all black belts. As if there wasn't enough pressure. We lined up and started the grading. The technique went well, but the whole time I was still trying to visualise my Kata. The worst thing is, as soon as you walked into the hall, you had to hand your Kata sheet over. So, there are no more chances to read it. If you couldn't remember it, tough!

We all then sit down and wait for our moment, respectively. It was nerve-racking! As I was sitting there waiting for my name to be called aloud by the instructor, from what seemed like an ever-growing list. Suddenly, the Kata just completely disappeared from my head. It was like someone had wiped a hard drive. I made the grave error of watching someone else perform theirs, which was strongly advised against, as it made you forget your own. That's what happened to me. I was sitting there wretched, hoping my name didn't get called out. Rummaging around in my head, frantically trying to remember any of the moves I had spent months reciting. For the life of me, I couldn't recall them. I just kept hitting a wall of blackness every time I thought about it. Then, by some miracle the memory abruptly hit me, and I remembered the first move, it all flooded back into my brain. I breathed a huge sigh of relief, put my head down, shut my eyes, and zoned back in. I never looked up again. I replayed the moves in my head over and over. About five or six names flew by. Then I was up. I nervously walked up towards the front to face all the black belts to perform my Kata. Much to my relief, I smashed it! I wasn't bothered about what came next. Even the sparring! Until the second round started... My adrenaline was relatively contained after it had peaked on the kata. Then it spiked again; I still had four more rounds to do. But this time I was hyper-aware that Jason was prowling around with his gloves on, ready to go. I had heard the stories about him and knew he was one tough bastard.

It looked like he was preoccupied with some younger students on the other side of the room. So, I thought I'd gotten away with it. Then he popped up in front of me and said, "right, me next". I smiled and nervously replied "okay". Inside, I was thinking, Oh fuck! I had my minute of rest and the round started. I thought I'd try out this new kick I'd been working on. You double up a roundhouse kick by aiming at the leg and then up to the head, without fully retracting it. I caught him on the side of the temple,

I was more shocked than he was. After I had displayed this clearly on my face, he proceeded to beat seven shades out of me. I immediately regretted the brief moment of showcasing my newly acquired skill. The worst part was, no one believed me that I caught him with a kick to the head, and I am sure no one believes me to this day. I don't make up random stories to look good. If I had done that, I wouldn't have told you the bit where I got my head smashed in afterwards.

I got a good mark and was proud of myself for once. Even Jason praised me after the grading and said my kata was well executed and thought out. He wasn't one to bestow any niceties if they weren't warranted, so it meant a lot. I even got congratulations from my mum. She and my dad got me a card saying well done. I think it was a bit of a relief for them, as they noticed a huge change in me, as I had some form of direction for the first time in years! Scott and Danielle had managed to attain their purple belts, respectively. So, it was a great night all around. I was already thinking about the next grade and asking questions. I saw what they had done and felt confident that I could pull it off once the time came.

Unfortunately, a few weeks down the road, Danielle noticed pain in her hips and had to go to the hospital for a check-up. She was told she had a form of arthritis in both hips and was unable to continue kickboxing. It was devastating news; it had a knock-on effect as well, because Scott didn't want to continue without her, and that meant I wasn't able to attend classes anymore. They were my means of transport at the time as I didn't drive, and there was no one else available that could take me. It was a bitter blow for all of us. It was a real shame because it replaced weed for me. I know that sounds bizarre, making that correlation, but it was a welcome distraction for someone who has an addictive personality.

In the summer of 2010, and without Kickboxing giving me the much-needed outlet and direction I craved. I fell back into the old habit of going out and drinking again. I was still smoking fags quite heavily and knew that the next gradings were going to be very difficult from a cardio perspective anyway. That is how I rationalised it in my head—that it just wasn't meant to be—and I strolled back to Loserville. It had quite a big impact on my mental health at that time. I still had no understanding of my mental state and gradually became an angry little man all over again! Dad was withering away in front of my eyes. I was struggling and looked for any excuse to go out and get plastered. Anything to block reality! Rhian was suffering with my ridiculous paranoia over nothing, and my parents were willing for me to go back to kickboxing somehow. Before I knew where I was, Christmas was only a couple of weeks away. Another year had escaped me. I am in a poorly paid job doing window cleaning, and it's become very apparent that I am still dealing with the after-effects of giving up smoking weed. To make matters worse, I knew deep down dad didn't have long left.

Despite everything my dad was going through, the man would not rest or sit down for longer than an hour. He spent weeks trying to fix an old table and chairs in the garden that my sister Tracey had given him. They were a bit battered and rotted, but it was a project for him that kept his mind occupied. Only for all of it to be destroyed that winter in a horrific storm. I could have cried for him, as he had no money and grafted so hard just so he could have a bit of garden furniture. A few days later, my friend Scott arrives unannounced at the door carrying a big package. He brings it through the porch-way. It's a brand-new table and chairs for my dad. My old man cried his eyes out because of the gesture, and I wasn't far behind. It's an in-joke now between Scott and me. I always tell him when we have a rare drink these days, thanks for the picnic table. But, being real, that is a testament to who he is, underneath all the inappropriate jokes and false lack of empathy.

October 2010, and Dad gets admitted to the hospital. Things are not looking good at all. My mum, Tracey, and I go to visit him. Everyone is standing there moping and very upset. He's got so many tubes sticking out of him that he looks like something out of a sci-fi film. I decide to break the tension with some ill-timed dark humour. I lean over, kiss him, and then gently whisper. I'm fucking glad I haven't bought your Christmas present yet, that would have been a complete waste of money wouldn't it. Which immediately got met with a "fuck off" from my dad and a slightly horrified look, coupled with a wry smile. Naturally, we're all fearing the worst. We weren't sure whether he will make it out of the hospital at this stage. After spending the night, they manage to stabilise him, and he ends up coming home. Unfortunately, the cancer had spread throughout the rest of his body. There was no further treatment that could realistically be administered to prolong his life. Although that horrendous news was devastating to hear, it wasn't a shock, just the cruel reality of mortality. He was very frail, and I don't think any of us thought he would see Christmas.

When we got dad home, he was barely able to do the basics. Within a month, he found himself back in the hospital. Which he was less than happy about. He desperately wanted to go to the Lion's Hospice, who had looked after him so well during his entire time with the Big C. The hospital said it wasn't possible as he was so weak, that if they tried to move him, he would likely pass away in the Ambulance. My dad, against his will, begrudgingly accepted what they were saying, and we all convinced him he was in the best place. 17th of November 2010 at 12:27 p.m. my beloved dad, Ron, sadly passed away. I, Tracey, mum, and Rhian were in the room with him. My friends Rick, Adam, and Rick's girlfriend at the time, Wendy, were just outside the door. Rick had upped and left work and said, sack me if you want, I'm going. I'll never forget that as long as I live. Adam wasn't working at the time, he jumped straight in the car and got there in 15 minutes. I'll forever be appreciative of their efforts to be there for me. I am so glad I was there for my old man when he transitioned to the other side. Even though he was barely conscious and struggling to breathe, I held his hand and said, "Dad, I'm sorry. You know I love you, don't you? I'm sorry I didn't do more". I felt the faintest squeeze on my right hand. He acknowledged what I said, and as nice as that was, it haunts me to this day that even though he was barely alive, his breathing was rapid and shallow, he still found something within him to let me know he heard what I said. To feel his hand slip away from mine like that broke me. I have never really recovered from that moment. I don't think I ever will!

I still find it hard to accept that life can be so cruel and evil at times. When he faded away, I sat there and wept in utter disbelief. We were all inconsolable. Feeling the last piece of life leave his frail and withered body was horrible. I couldn't hold his hand for long, knowing that his soul had left. I didn't expect any words from anyone, there's nothing anyone can say, is there? We all dejectedly made our way out of the hospital. I remember standing outside, traumatised by what had just happened. I could hear and see people talking, but I couldn't make out what was going on. I felt like I was underwater and slowly drowning. It was one of the worst feelings I have ever experienced in my life. Something was calling me back into the hospital. It was like I was being dragged back in against my will. Although I never wanted to step foot in there ever again! I followed whatever was pulling me towards it. So, I turned to everyone, and said I'd be back shortly. I went to the room where my dad lay, motionless. I was completely shell-shocked. I looked through the window of the door, then slowly opened it. I know this sounds crazy, but I tried waking him up. I said, "Dad, Dad." I couldn't touch him, as I didn't want to feel what I knew deep down was now just a dead body. There was no response. I walked around the bed and stood next to him, just looking at him, willing him to open his eyes - he didn't. It then dawned on me that my old man was never coming back. I didn't stay long, as it was too painful to see him losing his colour, becoming grey and ashen. That was starting to play on my mind even more than when his hand slipped away from mine. I left that room a different man.

I headed back through the hospital corridors, which now felt like they were closing in and suffocating me. As I got back outside, my mum and Tracey were still weeping, understandably. After that point, there is total caliginosity. I can't remember who took me home, or anything about the journey. So, I would rather take this moment to talk about my dad and give you an insight into who he was. Ron, as most of you will remember him, was a character. He was truly one of a kind. The impact he had on me and many other people's lives is unfathomable! Some of the things I have written about him previously, may have made you prejudge him earlier in the book. Don't be fooled, He was a gentle, loving, kind, and generous man. He was quite tough on us as kids, but he had a hard upbringing himself. My dad was from old-school Bermondsey, London. You won't find more genuine, salt of the earth people. But they don't suffer fools gladly, and my dad was no different. One thing my old man didn't have much of up until I was about six years old was money; he'd give me all the time in the world he could to make up for it. You can't buy time, that was always more valuable than money to me. No matter how tired he was, he would play football or tennis with me. Which I was too young to appreciate at the time, but I appreciate it now dad. He was full of banter and jokes and would always play the clown, to either wind people up, or get people laughing. He was a chronic piss-taker and forever the life and soul of any room he walked into. It wasn't to be showy or attention-seeking; far from it. It was purely because everyone always seemed so miserable to him and took life too seriously.

There was a disconnect, with him being a Londoner, living in Kent. Kentish people aren't quite as laid-back. So many people found him irritating, especially in Meopham. He would always call out every Tuesday when the bingo was on, despite not even playing. He did it just to wind them all up, as a few of them had sticks up their arses for want of a better phrase. The first number would get called out on the night, and he'd shout "HOUSE"! All the players would turn and sigh. He just couldn't help being a practical joker. It was inbuilt in him. He also used to wind me up; I regret snapping at him now, as it was just a laugh, but he had my card and knew he could pull it at any time. I remember one of the most classic moments when my dad went above and beyond to get a laugh, when we were in Spain. For some reason, he had the bright idea to run across the road and take his fedora hat off and pretend to be a homeless man. He held it out, begging for money. We all just stood there in disbelief. Some of us were laughing; others virtually ran for it. Within 30 seconds, a lady walked past and threw a couple of pesetas into his hat. He said, Gracias, then came back over the road, laughing his head off! I mean, it shouldn't come as a shock from a man who had his wake while he was still alive, I'm sure!

My dad would take great enjoyment embarrassing me outside my school by playing up and shouting across the car park. One time, I was running late. He drove me into the parking bay at a stupid speed which was so unlike him. There was a group of travelers standing in the way near where he was going to park. I said, "Dad, STOP! They're travelers, you'll get me a kick-in". To which he replied. "They'll be travelling on my bonnet if they don't get out of the fucking way." Back then, that wasn't funny. Today, I am rolling up, writing this. Brilliant! I wasn't the only victim where things of this nature were concerned. He went to pick up his best friend at an airport once; dressed up to the nines with a board that had his best friend's full name written on it, in large letters. He proceeded to scream at him at the top of his lungs. "COOEE RUSSELL, I'M OVER HERE" in the campest voice. While jumping up and down and waving frantically. You couldn't trust the guy; he was chaos in a bottle and never changed.

Even though he had cancer, he'd be the same, right up until the end of his life. He never once felt sorry for himself or ever lost his sense of humour. I think that's something everyone reading this can admire. Whether you knew him or not, he was a massive hit with all my friends. They worshipped the ground he walked on and found him hilarious. The prankster, the joker, the court jester. Whatever you want to call him. Quickly became the boy who cried wolf one day. It was the day of his heart attack, which I thought he was joking about. I stood over him, kicking him and saying these words, "Dad. Get up, stop fucking about, you twat!" He was genuinely having a heart attack on the living room floor and asking for an ambulance. Luckily, my mum was there; otherwise, I'd probably still be kicking him now.

I didn't realise how alike we were; nowadays I can see myself slowly morphing into him. I don't mind at all. If I could be half the man he was, I'd be an extremely proud and fulfilled man. Many people make comments, drawing parallels between my dad and I. That I look like him now, that my sense of humour is very similar. I miss him dearly to this day and am heartbroken that he didn't get the chance to see me sort my life out. Well, who has ever really gotten their shit together? I'm trying my best! I wanted to go on and live in a way that will honour him and not disappoint him. Unfortunately, it would take me a mere 5 years after his passing to do so. The name Ron is often spoken and is forever present. The man himself is still very much in people's memories over a decade later. That means he still lives on. As long as his name continues to reverberate fondly around the circles of the people he knew; the memory of my great father will never perish. The approach my dad had to adversity and life, in general, is the bravest I have ever witnessed. The fight to go on for his loved ones was nothing short of extraordinary! We have his voice forever recorded on a CD he made just before he died. It is priceless, as it doesn't just encapsulate the music he loved, it embodies his soul as well. You can hear the pain in his voice when he's trying to sing for the last time. That, for me at least, is the most real thing I have ever heard. I have taken many things from my old man, and despite him thinking I didn't listen, I always did. I may have pretended I wasn't at the time and come across as nonchalant and dismissive. But I took things on board. I know somehow, somewhere, he's overseeing me and smiling down. I think it's a beautiful way to end this chapter. On a high note, and one that carries the spirit of a wonderful dad, husband, grandad, friend, and above all, a truly great man who will be forever in our thoughts and sorely missed. R.I.P Dad. You certainly left your mark. Ronald Brian Gollop, (28/12/1936) - Forever!

Chapter 9

The Aftermath

After a horrendous ending to 2010, losing my dad a month before Christmas was tough on us all. It would have been all too easy for me to fall off the wagon and use it as an excuse to start the weed up again, or drink more. I chose to do the complete opposite. Around four months into the year, I decided it was time to give up smoking. I thought if I could do it now, then nothing could stop or derail me. I went to the local doctor's surgery and asked for help. The nurse provided me with a prescription for Champix pills. She said I was lucky that I decided to try and quit at the age of 27, as my lungs would still have a chance to make a full recovery. Armed with my new (legal) drugs for a change.

I walked home with a new frame of mind and, a positive attitude. It was probably the least ideal conditions to achieve this new lofty goal I had set for myself. No one thought I would do it, and although that played on my mind quite a bit, it also pissed me off enough to go and prove all the doubters wrong. Like I did when I quit smoking weed. I told my friend Adam about it, he said, "I'm sure my brother Sean took those pills and became suicidal on them". The doctor did warn me that 1 in 10,000 people have that reaction, it sent shivers down my spine, that I knew someone this had happened to. Sean had to go back to the doctors to get another drug to counteract them. With my family history, I was initially too scared to take them and the pills remained in the kitchen cupboard for three months. I had tried many times off willpower alone and never cracked it. Then one day, I thought, you know what, I'm going to at least try! If it all goes awry, then I can go and get the pills to counteract the Champix. The other side effects that were much more likely, were nightmares and dizzy spells during the day. It wasn't an ideal situation when you're a window cleaner. 1 in 1,000 would experience those side-effects. So, I kept a close eye on what was going on with my body. A week in, I did feel a bit weird. Food started tasting slightly different, and I wasn't sparking up as often.

In the second week, I had to introduce a second stronger pill. That was when fags were smelling like they used to before I started (horrible), and my appetite was measurably better. I was smoking, on average, two to three fewer cigarettes a day. It was nice to see progress, I was quietly confident that if I was going to have any serious side effects, they would have already happened. Then I started getting bad dizzy spells. Sometimes, I had to clutch onto the ladder for dear life, hoping I wasn't going to fall off and smash myself to bits. I dealt with that ok, I was just relieved I wasn't getting any suicidal thoughts. Or having any horrific nightmares.

However, one night, that all changed. To this day, I am almost certain I had an out-of-body experience. Stay with me here. I know there's some eye-rolling going on; hear me out! I was fast asleep. I think these pills were knocking me out at night to some degree. Then, the most vivid, nightmare/out-of-body experience started to occur. I remember my dad telling me he had one himself years ago. It seemed now that it was my turn. I felt myself float up out of bed, it was cold in my room. Everything had this Icey sheen to it. I slowly stood up straight to a standing position, although, my feet never reached the floor. I was floating, about three inches off the ground. My eyes appeared to remain shut; I was observing this situation unfold. My bedroom door slowly started to crack open without me touching it. I then began to lean out of my room into the corridor. This foreboding tenebrosity swelled throughout the house, I felt an ominous presence almost smothering me. I then realised the cupboard and bedroom doors were a blindingly bright white. It was like I was in my own horror film. I floated through the landing, my mum and dad's bedroom door opened for me. I briefly paused and then proceeded to hover into their room. My mum was fast asleep, my dad sitting bolt upright, wide awake, with a roll-up in his mouth as usual, whilst reading the paper. He peered over the top of his glasses at me and said, "are you alright, son"? I said, "yeah, I'm ok, Dad. I was just checking in on you". He then replied, "I'm going to sleep now. I am shattered". With that, I said goodnight, and then, rather than turn around to leave, I floated backwards out of their bedroom. As soon as I reached the landing, I felt a cold chill travel through me. Then, out of absolutely nowhere, their bedroom door slammed shut violently! It deafened me and nearly came off the hinges. I was then ripped backwards by some unknown force through the landing, as if I were flung out of a catapult. All the cupboard doors in the hallway were slamming shut. I couldn't work out why they were open in the first place. Even the backdoor was open until the same happened, and it crashed shut. I was then sucked back into my bedroom by this undeniable force, I can only compare to that of a giant vacuum cleaner. My bedroom door closed so hard it nearly got ripped off. I felt myself land on my bed, as if I had dropped from a height. As soon as my body hit the mattress, I woke up and gasped for air. I couldn't breathe at all. I was hyperventilating and soaked, dripping with sweat, I thought I'd pissed my bed. I turned around, and sheets were ringing wet. The T-shirt I had on changed colour. I jumped up to turn the light on, in a completely panic-stricken frenzy. I couldn't make sense of what just happened. Was it real? Did I dream it? I cautiously opened my bedroom door and looked out into the hallway. Then it hit me. I suddenly recalled talking to my dad. Then my rational mind kicked in and was like, what in the fuck am I talking about? He's dead! But I know for a fact that I just spoke to him. I had this internal argument with myself for a couple of minutes.

I slowly walked up to my parents' bedroom door and opened it. It was so real, I had to check. I couldn't leave it. Much to my disappointment, dad wasn't there, just my mum snoring. I welled up and tried desperately to regain some form of normality. I walked back into my room and changed my bed. I had to flip my mattress; it was that bad. Once I'd done that, I got into the shower. I was all clammy, in a state of shock and disillusioned by the event. All I could keep thinking was, that I had spoken to my dad. I know I did! It was far too real for it to have been a dream. Even today, I truly believe that I tip-toed over the line between this reality and the next. The reaction of my body wasn't that of your standard nightmare, and I have had plenty! None had this level of intensity, or self-awareness as it was taking place as this one did. It looks like the Champix pills didn't let me down. Was it that simple? Was it just the pills? I am not so sure. Astral projection is something that I became aware of after the event, and it wasn't too dissimilar to that from what I had read. But I was asleep at the time, wasn't I? I suppose it's going to have to be one of those unanswered questions I have to live with and accept. Even though that whole experience harrowed me for years afterwards, to share it is quite special. Maybe I did achieve astral projection that night. I'm quite content for it to never happen again, it put the fear of God into me, I haven't ever felt that out of control in my entire life. Even to this day, nothing has come close.

I was three quarters of the way into my nightmare pills, that horrific experience didn't deter me one bit. A week or so later, I was smoking around three fags a day and chucking most of each one away. The toughest part, as most ex-smokers will testify, is when you go out for a drink. My friends were getting to the point of refusing to give me fags or let me have a drag on theirs. One weekend we were all out having a few beers, I pleaded with my mate to let me have a few drags on his cigarette. After a lot of pestering and moaning, he gave in and said, "I don't know why you're doing it. You have nearly quit"? I took two or three drags and felt sick. From that point on, I knew that was it for me. The rest was just a placebo of having one with a beer. It did take me a while to get used to that notion, as I was a much heavier smoker when I was drinking than when I wasn't. But who isn't? It was almost exactly a year from the day of my dad's passing. I could finally say I was smoke-free. It took me a while, but I got there. One of the incentives to quit was to get myself back into kickboxing, as I had a goal to pursue.

At this point, I wasn't close to Ross. I was just another kickboxer who had walked through the door one day. I decided to message him on Facebook, and tell him I was coming back in a few months, and that I had stopped smoking. I was going to get fit to come and get that black belt. I am sure he had heard it all before. But I was very serious and almost with immediate effect, started training at home. I left as an orange belt and I struggled massively with the fitness that grading required. I had high hopes; I wanted to come straight back in and double grade, which wasn't very realistic. It was a massive target to set for myself, but it was one I had my sights set on, and I wasn't about to let it go. Although I was still going out on the weekends, I was training throughout the week with every spare moment I got. I was very eager to prove to myself that I could do what was required and make my dad proud, just in case he could be witnessing my journey from the other side. Which was something that got unexpectedly answered for me one day many years later.

Upon my return to kickboxing and a few lessons in, Ross asked me how I was getting to training. I said I was getting a cab to and from my house. He asked how much it was costing me; it was over double the amount it cost me to train. He realised then, how serious I was about Kickboxing, and offered to at least take me home to save me money. He started picking me up as well after a couple of weeks, I think he was impressed by my dogged determination to succeed. I could fully understand his scepticism about me quitting smoking and coming back. Sometimes when I got in the car, he'd ask me if I started again because I stunk of fags. It was because my mum was smoking non-stop all day, the house and all my clothes, unfortunately, reeked of smoke. My training would go on to prove I was getting fitter and fitter by the week. Just as well, as grading was every four months, and I had just missed one which was quite annoying, as I was desperate to progress quickly and make up for lost time.

Those four months flew by, I was starting to feel those unrelenting nerves I had back in 2009. When I first walked through the doors. I secretly hoped that I would be chosen to double grade. The next one is green, the one after is purple. Ross approached me and said, "do you want to double grade? You've been training while not present in class, and I can tell you're ready for it". I was beaming! The word yes immediately fell out of my mouth. I did think for a moment, what have I just done?

Although, that was only a fleeting thought. I started to prepare meticulously, as I always did. The pressure was on, and I wasn't about to let myself down after all the hard work I had put in behind the scenes. I think I thrive off pressure to be honest. If I have something that puts a little fear in me, it makes me feel alive! The penultimate night came around quickly, and before I knew where I was, it was time. I hated grading nights as the nerves were extremely intense; the fear of failure used to eat away at me. In hindsight, it kept me sharp and ready for whatever the night bestowed upon me. It was a busy club at this time, there were plenty of eyes on me, which made it all the more nerve-racking. Luckily, the night went well, without any mishaps. I passed with flying colours; the relief poured out of me. If I remember rightly, I received an 89% pass mark. As soon as I walked out, I was already thinking about the blue belt. Naturally, I did let myself enjoy the moment, however brief it was. Probably a day or two. I now recognise that despite what I achieve, I never let myself rest on my laurels; it's straight on to the next thing. Even back then, when my life was a mess, I still managed to achieve what I put my mind to. Unfortunately, outside of kickboxing, that focus was seldom present.

I was still flitting in between jobs and incapable of holding anything down, due to either resenting all my time being taken away from me, or hating the job itself. Then something caught my eye on a job website. A salesman? I thought, why not? I'll try and get an interview. Not for one minute did I think I would get a call. The next day my phone rings and I am asked to come in for an interview. I approached it with a care-free attitude, as I thought I didn't stand a chance. I had no experience in that field. So, why would they hire me? Inevitably, I think that stood me in good stead. I flew through the interview stages and went straight into an observation day, to see how it was done. Ah. Door-to-door sales. I immediately thought, No way! I can't do this. These guys surely can't make a penny doing this stuff, can they? How wrong I was. The boss was raking it in, I was utterly bemused. How was he achieving it? Between £64,000 and £67,000 a year! It was mainly a commission-based role as well. Impressive stuff. It was like a license to print money. So, I went along for a few days and watched him on the doors. Much to my surprise, he smashed it, every single day, without fail. It gave me some belief - but there's a huge difference between watching someone else do it and doing it yourself. On the last observation day, Mick, the manager said, "Are you ready? Why don't you give it a go"? I had been practicing the pitch he gave me, and summoned up some courage to knock on my first door. I took a deep breath and approached what looked like a winner. I stood there for 30 seconds. No one answered. But the seal was broken. I marched on immediately to the next door. I nearly got a lead on my first interaction. I was shocked and thought, right then, I can do this. I took the job. after a few weeks, I was getting leads left, right, and center. Somehow, it just seemed to click with me.

The after-effects from smoking weed were finally subsiding, and my confidence was slowly coming back. No way on God's green earth would I have attempted a job role like this before. But here I was doing door-to-door sales, commission only, and taking a chance. It was quite a ballsy move and the job also got me fit by proxy, because of all the walking I was doing each day. I settled in well, and got on with everyone who worked there. They were a good bunch of lads and the main boss of my branch was a Millwall fan. I think played a role in me getting the job in the first place. It was nice to feel part of a team for once and not be an outcast. After a few months, I was pushing Mick my team leader, for the top place on the leaderboard for quotes and sales. I managed to put all the negativity that was absorbing me in my home life to the back of my mind and crack on with the job. Unfortunately, mum's alcoholism had gotten considerably worse since dad passed. She fell further into the chasm of self-neglect, there was nothing I, or anyone else could do about it. I just had to keep focusing on my life, no matter how hard that was. I managed to drag myself through the year. My blue belt grading was coming up in September, so, I had to be zoned in. I knew it was going to take every ounce of fitness I had to be successful. When grading night finally arrived. I got lumbered sparring five rounds with a guy called Naz, who was a nightmare to fight and much bigger than me. He outweighed me by a good 20 kg. I got my head jabbed off for all five rounds. I managed to pull off an amazing Kata and smash the technical side of the grading, along with ground fighting. I received a pass mark of 91%. I put in the time to train and practice outside of the club. I knew there was no way you could just turn up for two sessions a week and expect to pass. 2012 flew by! With 2013 around the corner, I was determined to stay on a positive trajectory, keep myself fit, and hopefully retain my job for a change. Rhian and I were still relatively strong, despite my unpredictable nature and sometimes outlandish behaviour. Most of the time, I tried to burn the candle at both ends, party weekends as well as train kickboxing. It was going to be a big year commencing with my brown belt coming up, which would be the first time I fought full contact in a controlled environment. Having the physical outlet from martial arts was just about keeping my head above water. Although, it wasn't enough in itself to steady the ship. Then, six months into training really hard for my brown belt, I get shin splints. It was a disaster! I couldn't even walk properly, never mind run, or train.

With a hiatus from Kickboxing being forced upon me, and summer 2013 approaching; I retained a positive attitude and didn't fall off the rails this time. I knew shin splints took a while to heal, so I rested up and let my body go through the recovery process. I decided to channel my energy towards my music and start writing again. One afternoon when I was working on some new tracks, I opened YouTube to listen to some Hip Hop for inspiration. I played some Wu Tang Clan, then I noticed an advert for a live show they were playing at the famous Brixton Academy in London. Then I realised what date they were playing; 26th July, my Birthday! I was stunned; I felt it was a sign that I had to go and witness them live. I was low on funds at the time, so requested tickets as a birthday present. Rhian said she would get them for me, but when she tried to get the tickets, they had already sold out. I was devastated. What an experience that would have been, seeing my all-time favourite Hip Hop group, live on my actual birthday. On the 25th July, Rhian said I could open a present early. I thought it was a bit strange, I opened it to find two tickets to see Wu Tang Clan the next night. I was beside myself, and completely overwhelmed with excitement and disbelief.

We arrived at Brixton Academy an hour early, I was so nervously anticipating Wu Tang's entrance. The lights dimmed; the room filled with expectation. I shuffled my way closer to the front of the stage. The great thing about Brixton Academy is that the floor is slanted, so your vision is rarely blocked by the person in front of you. It has always been one of my favourite venues to watch live music for that reason. We heard a slight commotion coming from the back of the stage, then a muted light turned on. Shadows started appearing in the background. The crowd began to notice, and they started chanting. All of a sudden, they burst onto the stage and kicked it off with one of their most well-known songs. The place lit up; it went into absolute bedlam. People were flying everywhere, the place felt like it was charged with electricity! I have never seen anything like it. A part of me wanted to go mad, another part of me was completely in awe at what I was witnessing. But for the most part, I went crazy. The atmosphere grabbed you, there was nothing else you could do. The initial kick-off to the show calmed, after the first song was over. I noticed that Method Man wasn't on the stage. I thought, oh well, eight out of nine members showed up, that isn't bad. Then I heard the track M.E.T.H.O.D. MAN come on. Then from behind the dimly lit background, he flew onto the stage. Everyone screamed, and he absolutely killed it. What a start to the show. It was so iconic, it was unreal! Even Rhian was bouncing up and down.

Halfway through the gig, I noticed Raekwon had a bottle of Courvoisier in his hand. He was dancing around the stage while rapping and seemed to be having the time of his life. I was trying to make eye contact with him. I had by that point, gotten a bit further to the front, and he was standing near the edge of the stage. He looked out into the crowd, he appeared to be looking in my direction. I made a fist and hit my chest and gave him a salute of respect. He could have been looking over at any one of the twenty or thirty people around me, but he did the same back. That moment has stuck with me forever! He then proceeded to walk over, point me out, and try to hand the bottle to me. Security ruined it and blocked him from doing so, which seemed to piss him off. He began pushing them away. It nearly broke out into a fight. Nevertheless, being acknowledged by one of the greatest rappers to walk the planet and nearly sharing a bottle with him, is something I hold dear to this day. Over a decade later, it is still the best night of my life and is going to be nearly impossible to top. I don't think there was a person that I didn't tell about that evening. It was a good way to have a final blow-out. I didn't party quite as hard after that gig; I was slowly but surely getting back to full fitness. Plus, I had the slight issue of my biggest grading to date quickly approaching.

A couple of weeks later, Ross and I are having a conversation about setting a date for my brown belt grading. For the next few months, I was a bag of nerves, it wasn't just a grading this time. There was an essay to write on the pros and cons of Kickboxing as well. This was where things got quite serious, and if you weren't super fit and mentally ready, there was no way you would pass. I remember the drive there that night. I had no clue who I would be fighting. I was a bit worried it would be one of the bigger guys. I didn't want to get a pasting from a bloke twice my size. I nervously sat in the passenger seat of Ross' car. I asked who I would be fighting. He said I would be facing Callum, a younger guy, but at least my size. He had been a black belt for around three years. So, he was a very decent fighter and technician. It was hard to know which bit to be most nervous about at this stage. When we turned up, there were only a handful of others present. Full contact wasn't allowed to be witnessed by anyone of a lower grade due to what could happen. On the technical side, I smashed it out of the park. I breathed a sigh of relief. But there was still so much to do. The Kata, was a prewritten one by the top instructors. It's the first time since the red belt, that I had to follow a set of moves I hadn't written myself. You had no room for error!

Up next, was 5-Rds of "semi-contact" sparring. There were multiple moments where you'd receive a hard shot from someone, to indirectly prepare for what was coming, and test you to see if they could get you to lash out and lose your temper. Which would result in an immediate failure. It was mental warfare. That was followed by three rounds of full-contact fighting. Ross gave me a pep talk as he smeared the Vaseline on my brow. I had completed the majority of the grading. It all rested on full-contact. Although extremely nervous, there was no way I was ever going to back out. I'd rather have been knocked out, then walk away. The fight started, and Callum wasn't messing around. He hit me with a few solid punches, and then he went down to my legs with some heavy kicks. After two rounds, I started to feel the pace, especially as I had already done 5-Rds of Semi-Contact prior, and Callum was as fresh as a daisy. I can't recall what round it was, but Callum hit me with the same combo a few times. Due to my inexperience in full contact, I fell for it. Hook, line, and sinker. He then hit me with three hard low kicks to the left thigh with his reverse leg.

If anyone reading this has had a shine bone to the leg, full power more than a few times, you'll know that the pain is quite intense! I knew I had to do something. I couldn't just stand there getting whooped for the sake of it. As he unleashed another barrage of punches to my head, I covered up and decided enough was enough. I threw the biggest overhand right I have ever thrown in my life and hit him flush on the nose. It made this emphatic popping sound and echoed throughout the hall. I thought I had broken his nose. Everyone gasped, I looked up, expecting him to be either on the floor or at least wobbling. Much to my surprise, it didn't look like I had touched him. He just marched forward and kept fighting, a testament to his toughness. I made it through the 3-Rds, we both embraced afterwards. I had passed. If I remember correctly, I received a 92% mark, which I was over the moon with. Callum said to me after the fight that he couldn't believe I didn't go down and called me a tough bastard. I echoed praise back his way. "How did that right hand not move you? I couldn't understand how that overhand right barely registered with you"? I was quite banged up and very sore for a good couple of weeks after. It makes you appreciate what these professional fighters have to endure. This wasn't something I'd be doing every couple of months like those guys. It is incredible what they put their bodies through. It was a great end to 2013, and I took some well-deserved time out from training and enjoyed

Christmas that year. It's a shame I didn't stay on this positive path for too much longer.

Chapter 10

The Downward Spiral

I was coming off a reasonably positive 2013. Unfortunately, I didn't capitalise on my recent success and got lured back into an unsavoury way of life. It stemmed from one random Thursday night with my friend Jon. (I'm not blaming him at all.) We always went to the same pub in the village, but this particular night he suggested a pub up the road. I had never been in there, as it had a reputation for being a bit of a dive. He persuaded me to give it a go. So, I thought, why not? As we arrived, I was quite surprised. It looked genuinely nice and had no riff-raff in there whatsoever. I had heard horror stories over the years, but new management had taken over, and they had turned the place around dramatically. We went to order our drinks, much to my surprise my friend Ruby was working behind the bar. Many hours later, we still found ourselves in there, absolutely hammered! Having a good old catch-up. From that night on, The Winchester became my local boozer. Unbeknownst to me at the time, I would go on to make some good friends, some of whom I still talk to today. Jon and I started going up there on the odd weeknight and then began to pop in on Friday's and Saturday's. As the weeks passed by, other people we knew started drinking there. It was a matter of months before we took the place over. There are honestly too many people to name one by one. But on a good night, there were over twenty of us. It was mayhem, and it wasn't long before we all became close friends. When everyone got comfortable with each other, the question, do you do coke? came up. I was never one for Class A drugs. I had dabbled in the past but I never really understood the fascination with it. That was all about to change very quickly!

One of the guys brought some out with him one weekend. What started with being a few innocent pints up the pub on a Thursday night, then became ten pints of lager and bags of white stuff every weekend. To be honest, it got ridiculous! To the point that we were all ushered to one side of the bar most weekends so other customers could enjoy their night out. We were a rowdy bunch. We never caused any trouble; looked for fights or anything like that; it was always harmless fun. Albeit, loud fun! Jack behind the bar became a good friend, he was very patient with everyone, in all honesty. Jack and I are still very close to this day, and he's one of the people who made a huge difference in my life without really knowing it. Every weekend felt like things went a step further. Most nights tended to boil over past the pub, and We'd all usually end up going back to mine or someone else's house to keep the night going. Things never seemed to calm down, if anything, they got worse. We still managed to cause havoc and get out of control most weekends. One of my friends was doing lines off another mate's bald head at 2 am on a Tuesday night. I fell asleep on the toilet with my trousers around my ankles one night. Someone plummeted across the bar wiping out every stool in his path. People having their drinks spiked with MDMA. It all went on.

The pub wasn't the only place we partied. In fact, it was ten times worse was around my friends Lewis and Zack's parents' house. Numerous nights around there were legendary—far too many to mention or that I could possibly remember. But a few nights stick out in particular. The fact that I am still alive is astonishing! I'm truly grateful to be able to sit here and tell these stories. Admittedly, stories I am not very proud of. One memorable evening when I first tried MDMA instantly springs to mind. Scott and I were standing in the front room at patio doors leading towards the back garden, when Zack came strolling through with two scrunched-up balls of Rizla in his hand. He opened his palms, looked at Scott, and said, "do you want some of this? It's MDMA"! Without even blinking, Scott threw it in his mouth. I was shocked! Zack, looking slightly concerned, said "that's a big bomb for your first rodeo mate". Scott laughed and said, "Oh well, I've done it now". He probably got his inner confidence from the eight beers he had drank previously. I looked at him and said, Fuck it! You're not going alone mate, and I threw the other ball into my mouth without a care in the world. Also, having never done it before! It was a beautiful summers evening. Loads of us were out and partying, having a great night, and loving life like people in their twenties do. Around half an hour later, Scott comes up on the MDMA and immediately freaks out. He is sitting on the floor rocking back and forth, wearing a winter jacket and flip-flops while literally pulling his hair out. Most of us thought he was going to have to go hospital. Scott was in a complete state of disarray and didn't know his arse from his elbow.

I looked at him and thought, great, that's going to be me in about five minutes. Then I thought, no way, you can't think like that. It's a negative mindset, and everyone is different. Just ride it out, and it'll all be fine. Lo and behold, five minutes go by, and I feel this warm, tingling sensation in my toes. I thought, oh, here we go! Within seconds, pins and needles rush up my body aggressively. Then this euphoric feeling hits me. My god, it felt amazing! I had never felt something so intense in my life. I am not condoning drugs. Like all highs, there comes lows. You'll find out just how low, in the next few chapters of my life. I felt compelled to move; I couldn't sit still. Scott was in a bad way. I separated from the crowd and I went into the front room, where the Drum and Bass was blaring out and started raving like I was at the Ministry of Sound. I didn't care who was watching or what they were saying. I was in my little bubble, feeling like I'd transitioned to a higher realm. It's amazing how the same thing can affect two people so differently. I think it was more a mindset than anything else. A part of me felt bad for not being there for my mate, but he already had five people standing around him, and I was no good to him as I was just as high as he was. So, I carried on having a great time. Eventually, after about an hour or so, they managed to calm him down. He went home with his tail between his legs, feeling a bit worse for wear. Like many nights around there, I don't remember how it concluded. All I know, is we all had a great time.

The best house party came later that year and was another night around Lewis and Zack's. I'll try to set the unbelievable scene.

Rhian and I turn up around 4pm. There are people everywhere! We walk through the back gate. There are plastic balls, hula hoops, illuminous paint, and a projector set up in the garden, the back of the house is lit up projecting music videos. It was like being at a festival. Even his parents were out the back, sitting on the picnic table, smoking weed and having a blast. They were both very chilled and welcoming—two of the loveliest people you could wish to meet. I took a seat at the table and had a few beers. There were lots of Class A drugs floating about, namely cocaine and MDMA. I had a couple of lines. Then someone handed me a ball of MDMA. I was sitting there, engaging in conversation for about an hour, then BOOM! It kicked in. I had to leave the table and go for a walk right away. If I had been in an environment, I wasn't comfortable with, maybe things could have easily gone the other way. Everyone was on a good vibe that night, and I was no different. After a few hours of enjoying the craziness that went on, with everyone covered in luminous paint, and plastic balls flying around the garden, with incredibly loud Drum and Bass blasting out. I wandered off, I was found standing in some bushes talking to myself. Or maybe I was talking to the tree? Genuinely, I'm not sure, even to this day, if I am being transparent. Zack said, "You ok, mate? Come on, Come back to the party." He grabbed my hand and ushered me back towards the front room. I was completely out of my box and not living in the world that everyone else was currently residing in. It wasn't too long before I once again wandered off aimlessly. This time, I was found playing real-life Tetris in their garage, lining up all their boxes in size and shape order. Zack came in and said "dude. What are you doing"? I turned around with a confused look on my face, and replied, "I don't know Zack to be honest"—and chuckled to myself. He guided me back to where everyone else was. But that wasn't the end of my antics by a long shot.

Rhian and I left the party at around 3 a.m. As soon as I arrived back home, I was adamant that we had left Zack and his missus outside the hairdressers. I was pleading with Rhian, that we had to go back and pick them up because they were stranded. She burst out laughing and told me I was making no sense, and that we couldn't go back because our lift had already driven off. It was at least a 45-minute walk. I was seriously contemplating walking all the way back, due to the story I had made up entirely from imagination. There were no hairdressers where they lived, and they weren't stranded! I turned around to Rhian and said, "don't panic. I have an idea"! I took my phone out of my pocket, then started searching through my apps. Rhian asked me what the hell I was doing? I replied candidly, "I am going to teleport through my phone and go and get them". I was deadly serious! She managed to talk me down and finally get me into bed with no further dramas. I then started rambling about a hamster stuck in a wheel that had to be rescued. I was not on planet Earth at this point. Shortly after, I passed out, and I imagine much to the relief of Rhian. A few days later, I spoke to Zack. He said how genuinely concerned he was for me. His exact words were, "Mate, I genuinely thought you'd crossed over, and we weren't going to get you back". After that night, I had a sore jaw for six months. I would wake up, and my jaw would be aching where I had been clenching it in my sleep.

I was falling off the wagon again, and on a self-destruct mission due another nasty injury at Kickboxing. A torn groin! With the next grading being my Black Belt, which would be at least a year away. There was no rush to be fit. I decided this was the time to let loose! I just couldn't seem to stay on the straight and narrow for the life of me. I know now my mental health was in a seriously bad way. Although, at the time it didn't occur to me that I wasn't well. I just kept falling into substances to block out reality, and had the temerity to judge my mum for her drinking. We just affected people's lives in different ways I suppose. I didn't care about me and had little to no regard for my own well-being at all. There were nights I prided myself on doing the most drugs, drinking the most, and being the last man standing. It was like a badge of honour back then—ultimate stupidity! One night, I did so much Cocaine that not only did my nose close up, my windpipe started to close as well. I turned to Rhian and said, "I think I need to go to the hospital". In a concerned, shaky tone. She replied, "stop shoving that shit up your nose then, leave it out for tonight". I had an hour's break from it, and felt a lot better.

Then, like a complete idiot, I went straight back to it. I look at that "man" today and have nothing but contempt for him. A big part of me thinks I was trying to end my life in my own way.

Amongst all these shenanigans, Scott's Stag Do was just around the corner. A gaggle of us lunatics ended up in Butlins, of all places. Say what you will about Butlins - it was a great time. Lewis got kicked out on the first night for getting caught doing gear in the toilet, the muppet. But the rest of us enjoyed our stay in room 431. Which was being slowly but surely demolished. In the early hours of the next morning, I was being pushed around the room on a parcel trolley. Shit was everywhere! Someone's boxer shorts had been launched off the balcony, my friend Dave was trying to ring Babestation to talk to Tiffany. Someone rang the reception desk and asked for one of them to bring our underwear back. The lady politely, declined, and labelled us "fearless bastards'.' It was like a scene out of Hangover by the time we had to go home. But what a memorable stag Do that we all came away from relatively unscathed. surprisingly!

2014 became unrelenting! I was also going to The Den regularly to watch Millwall play, cleverly using that as another excuse to get out of my face. One weekend, a friend and I went to Bromley Sports Bar to watch them because we couldn't get tickets. He turned up at my house at 8:30 a.m. with a massive bag of Cocaine, a bag of MDMA, and a bottle of Champagne. We were wired from 9 a.m. drank the champagne before even setting foot outside of the house. Hoovered up a few lines each, and then went about our day. Millwall won that afternoon, so we stayed out afterwards to celebrate. By 4 p.m. we started on the Mandy. We were unashamedly passing the bag back and forth right in the middle of the pub. Before we knew where we were, the whole bag had gone. I got up to go the toilet, as I walked out, it hit me like a ton of bricks! I was a good ten pints in. Two bags of Cocaine up my nose and half a bag of MDMA. We had spent over £600 between us; it was game over for me. We missed the last train home, and couldn't afford a cab back. We were trying to find someone who could potentially pick us up at 1 a.m. Terry managed to get hold of his mate Rob, who was from our local town to come to Bromley and pick us up. He offered to drop us locally, but not all the way to our doors. Which was still a damn sight better than where we were. All he requested was a bit of petrol money, so we stopped off at a garage on the way back. We all jumped out, I ran around the back to have a piss, as I was busting! I came back, jumped in the car, and said, "Ah, that's better". Only to be met by two massive guys. The guy in the back said, "What are you doing, bruv? "His face was all scarred, and he looked at me like he was about to rip my throat out. The guy in the front turned around and looked at me as if he were just about to punch my head in. I was in the wrong bloody car! It was an identical silver estate, parked in the same place, but not the same one! Little did I know they had filled up and moved out of the way for this other car to get petrol. I was one, embarrassed, and two, worried I was about to get stabbed! I made my drunken apologies and calmly slid out of the car. Only to be met by Terry and his friend, almost crying with laughter. I said "let's get the fuck out of here pronto!"

Rob dropped us off, and we were still 8 miles away from home. Both of us hurriedly went through our phones. We were trying to figure out who could save us. It is nearly 3 a.m. It's hard to select someone from your phonebook at that hour who won't want to kill you. We chose our friend Gemma. She agreed to save us. We turned around and began to stumble our way to her house, in the attempt to save her a little time. Just as we approached the top of the road, the police drove past us. They spun around instantly and pulled over to talk to us, quizzing both Terry and I about what we were doing and where we were going. Luckily, we had nothing on us, just in us. We explained that we had got stranded and that a friend was currently on her way to pick us up. They could tell we weren't sober, but before the interrogation could go any further, Gemma drove around the corner. Great timing! We went back to hers and watched films on the sofa. How we didn't end up in prison or dead that day I honestly do not know. Again, mindless behaviour!

Looking back and assessing it from a grown-up and sober place today. I am honestly embarrassed of the man I used to be. I know I was obviously unwell mentally, and using substances as an escape route. It was inevitable that they'd be a breaking point at some stage, but I'll be honest, I felt untouchable. I'd had so many punches in the head at kickboxing, and put so many drugs through my body, that I genuinely thought I'd acquired invincibility. Going into 2015, my attitude was no different! If anything, it was getting worse. It was clear I'd got a problem with cocaine. I wasn't ever dependent on alcohol, but it featured heavily on the weekends more often than not. Even the odd mid-week session was becoming much more regular. I started noticing I was getting blackouts, and not your normal; oh, I can't remember how I got home from the pub last night. I mean serious blackouts, where I was losing 4 or 5 hours some nights, and people were relaying things I had no recollection of. I would often find myself waking up and not even being at home some mornings. If I'd had a row with Rhian or my mum I'd storm off in the early hours, being a total arsehole! One morning, I woke up in the local park, not remembering how I got there. A Golden Retriever walked past me and people were looking at me. Another time, I woke up under a tree, completely dumbfounded as to how I was there. I had to call up the friends I was out with and ask them what happened the night prior. I don't think they knew how bad I was at the time. This is the first time I have actually voiced it. We were all getting so drunk, they probably didn't pay much mind to it.

When I wasn't sleeping outside, I was either in a different room or passed out on the floor somewhere. I'd sleep, walk, and piss everywhere and cause nothing but aggro. Sometimes, I got quite nasty when drunk, especially if something didn't go my way and if Cocaine was involved. Which at the time was nearly every weekend. Then I was ten times worse! I was out of control, something had to give. Then, in May of 2015, it did! I lost my relationship, through my persistent outlandish behaviour. I done the scumbag thing and was unfaithful. I was up to my eyeballs in class A drugs and pissed out of my mind. No one makes good, conscious decisions in that state. That particular night, I was black-out drunk. I don't remember how I got home, or the vast majority of the evening. I'm not trying to justify these shitty actions. But I know I was spiked that night with MDMA.

Because I didn't specifically take it but knew the feeling, and one of my pints tasted funny earlier on in the evening. Regardless, I would finally go on to pay the ultimate price. Also, someone would do the same to me. Albeit consciously and by choice, multiple times. I got my due karma! I realised the person I had become. Drugs were destroying me, and I was destroying everything and everyone around me in the process. I sank into one of the darkest places I had ever been, and as you've already read, I have been to some horrible, dark places. That week, I sat down and started to write a suicide letter. I took myself down to my brother's grave. I uttered these words through floods of tears and a cracking voice. "I apologise for letting you down, but I'm unfortunately coming to see you early".

I made my way to the woods. Took my jumper off and I tied it around a tree and made a slip knot to put my neck through. It was solid for about 10 seconds. Then it sluggishly slipped off the branch, and I fell to the floor, crying my eyes out, thinking, what in the hell was going on? I just wanted to die and felt hopeless. It was all my fault—years of abusing alcohol and drugs, acting lawless, and never knowing when enough was enough! I took time off from work. I was still a salesman; I couldn't face having to pretend to be happy every day on the doors. It didn't help that most people at work were on it as well. The sales industry at that particular time was rife with coke. It wasn't just in films, trust me! It's a crazy environment to operate in. I sank into a deep depressive state. Jon was away in the Navy, and all the others that were in the immediate circle got divided. There was only one way out. A few weeks passed, and I couldn't bring myself to leave the house. When Jon finally came home, he said I should go and talk to someone. He thought I had P.T.S.D. It didn't matter what I did or where I went. I couldn't be alone, or with people. Some say you have to hit rock bottom to rebuild, and, my god, it didn't get much lower than that. I quit all drugs immediately! A decade later, I have not touched a single one since and never will ever again.

After about three weeks, I had to go back to work. I simply couldn't afford to be off. I had bills to pay. When I went back, I was a shell of my former self. All my confidence was gone! I couldn't give stuff away on the doors. I was on a bad downward spiral, and it was one I couldn't seem to get out of, no matter how hard I tried. When I did manage to get out of the house, which was rare. I ended up going back home after about two hours. I just couldn't bear being around crowds of people anymore. By proxy that turned out to be a good thing in the long run. I had to get myself a new job as well. I couldn't do door-to-door sales anymore. The lifestyle I had led up to that point had got the better of me, and my heart just wasn't in it, which was a real shame. I was quite a decent salesman and had a natural way of chatting with people. It wasn't an easy job by any means. But if you could crack it, it was incredible. You learn a lot about yourself and other people. Even Jamie Foxx once famously said that doing door-to-door sales for two years is equivalent to a four-year communications college degree. But the time had come, I had to get a job where I knew I would get a standard wage every week, even if it was a low paid one. The commission-based nature of sales made me more anxious, as I couldn't focus and get my mindset right to make sufficient money. Each week, the take-home wage was getting worse and worse. I simply wasn't earning enough to eat, never mind pay bills.

I went back to agency work temporarily. I got a placement in a warehouse. It was terrible pay, but desperate times called for desperate measures. I was still in a severe state of depression. luckily, it was an easy job. I could still just about do it each day and hide what I was going through. I decided to go back to kickboxing to help clear my head and try to regain the focus I once briefly had. I still wanted that black belt deep down. After a month or so of being back in the fold and sharpening up, Ross rang me, he was desperate for someone to cover him and teach as he got caught up at work and couldn't make it. He didn't want to let everyone down and cancel the class. I agreed to teach the lesson. I thought it would be a good to take my mind off things, although a part of me was dreading it as I had been out of practice for some time. When I turned up, I immediately noticed there were some new faces I didn't recognise, and I was a little bit nervous. After about 20 minutes I found my feet, and the class started going well. Maybe this was just what I needed...

That was the night I met Anna. I took a bit of a shine to her and didn't notice that I was spending more time teaching the group that she was in than the others. Despite my head being all over the place, I managed to deliver a decent lesson. When I got home, I noticed a message in my Facebook inbox. I secretly hoped it was her, but I didn't think for one minute that it would be. It was! Surprised, and quietly happy I replied. Although it had only been four months since my last relationship with Rhian and definitely on a massive rebound, I didn't push her advances away. I should have done. I was still such a state. I thought it could be an opportunity to find happiness again, and maybe it was fate. After a few messages back and forth and talking at Kickboxing for a couple of weeks to get to know each other, we decided to go on a date. I was very nervous and wasn't quite sure. She was older than me by seven years, had three kids, and was on the verge of getting divorced. There was a lot to consider, but I gave it a chance. I didn't want to write it off and not even try. We went to a pub reasonably local to me, on the way there, I said, "Look, I'm not going to pull any punches, I am a bit of a mess at the moment". I told her what I'd been through. It was a lot for anyone to consume. Especially seeing as we were still in the car on the way to the date. I thought if I divulged all of this information now, she would have a chance to run early before either of us got too attached. When we got there, I did have quite a few to drink because I hadn't dated in well over a decade. She was like, "bloody hell, you're packing them away, aren't you?" I apologised and said I was just a bit nervous. After the date, which went well. We got a little physical. As the next few weeks passed by, we began seeing each other properly.

Things were changing quite rapidly, and I wasn't ready for it. I was getting up and still feeling on the brink of suicide every day, but I hid it well. I kept going to work, teaching at Kickboxing, seeing Anna, and just basically hoping one day I wouldn't feel like killing myself. I waited for that day to come in 2015. I longed for it to be a possibility, and it never happened. Something had to give. I couldn't keep pretending I was okay. Smiling, joking, and laughing with people. While on the inside, I was nothing but a broken spirit carrying around a carcass. Anna had no idea!

Some of my friends knew I wasn't right, and my sister Tracey. But no one knew how bad things were. To give you an insight into my frame of mind around this time, most lunchtimes at work, I'd walk out of the warehouse and go up into the woodland surrounding the grounds. There was a train track, and a bridge that crossed it. I can't tell you the number of times I walked up there crying my eyes out, looking at the trains going by, thinking about jumping. Some days were closer than others. The suicidal thoughts I was experiencing were horrendous and far too frequent. I didn't even contemplate how bad it was, to be honest. I used to think of how many different ways I could end my life. What would be the quickest? What would be the least traumatic for my loved ones? Could there be a way of doing it and making it look like an accident? These things would regularly fly through my brain. I almost became obsessed with it. My number one goal in life was how I could end my life.

The drug taking and drinking you may have been thinking I was glorifying previously, doesn't seem so great now, does it? There is nothing more brutal than reality! You can be anywhere in the world, but you can't run away from yourself unless you aren't here anymore to run away from. Whenever I came home from work, I'd tumble into a dark pit of despair. I'd try to keep my mind as occupied as possible. Whether that be with my music, or other interests. But nothing could keep me from the demons that hunted me down. Sometimes, I'd just sit there and cry like a baby for hours. No one knew, especially Anna. I'd be texting her as if things were completely normal. When we had our video calls, I was cheery and full of zest. Little did she know, probably five minutes before, I was sitting there thinking of how I could kill myself. As the year was coming to an end, I knew deep down the tightrope I was walking had to snap, and I would plummet to the floor. Then I had a bright idea. One that made perfect sense in my tortured head. I planned to take my life on January 2nd, 2016. It would have been the 18th anniversary, of the date that my brother killed himself. At least people could grieve on the same day, and there would not be two separate occasions to mourn. Even writing this now, knowing full well that no one knows this, it still makes sense to a certain degree. Not to take my life, but the thought process behind it back then. Although it would make for a tragic story, I think that would have been easier on my sister Tracey, of all people. Or would it? I don't know. All I know for certain is I was close. Very close! You can get a razor's edge from death if you have real intent behind your actions. Unfortunately, the intent behind mine was real—too real! Then comes the list.

Chapter 11

Live or Die I Choose

January 2nd, 2016... I'm sitting at my computer desk. I draw a line down the center of a piece of paper. On the left side, it has a list of goals and things I wanted from life. On the right side, it says kill yourself! I hovered over that list for hours, battling with myself and trying to make my decision. Believe me, it wasn't easy at all. The fact you are reading this means I chose the right one. The list read, get a permanent job, or at least hold the existing one down. Attain your black belt in Japanese kickboxing, pass your driving test, and record my music. Amongst various other little bits and pieces. Nothing about addressing my mental health, which is now first on my list every year. It now it reads - keep your mental health in check. Which is a lot easier these days. I've found as close to peace as you can get here. I felt like there was unfinished business, despite the catalogue of bad choices I had made previously, and all the people I hurt. There are people out there who have done much worse and been given a second chance. More importantly, they've given themselves a second chance. I cut the right side off the piece of paper and stuck the left side up on the inside of my wardrobe. I adopted this attitude of fuck the world. I am going to try my best to right these wrongs and make myself a better person from this day on.

The journey began. Anna and I were around six months into dating, I was struggling with the fact that she was hard to reach and get close to. I thought it was me, and I was being petty, but it wasn't. I knew that Anna previously had bad breakups and was very guarded. I'm not about to sit here and lambast her for her wrongdoings, as I also made my mistakes and not to mention that in my opinion, it lacks the class. Relationships are very personal things. I could sit here and make many people look bad. How easy would that be to achieve? It's my book, and there is no rebuttal here. Everyone makes mistakes, and that's just life.

The ghosts of the past that haunted my soul were ever present, but I was determined to beat them and succeed. I had been training in kickboxing diligently since the end of 2015. I put all the syllabus sheets up on the back wall of the warehouse where I worked, so I could train during my lunch hour. I booked some driving lessons at the grand old age of 30! It was about time I pulled my finger out. I had a rough idea of how to drive, as I'd done a little bit on building sites and rode a motorcycle. So, there was slightly transferable skills from those.

I was nervous about my first lesson, but it went surprisingly well. The driving instructor asked me why it had taken me so long to start lessons. I said it'd been a curse. Every time that I attempted to start them, I have either lost my job or something has gone wrong and stopped me. I said, "you watch, I'll probably lose my job now," and laughed. I must have spoken that into existence, as the week after I got laid off. I couldn't believe it! I was easily one of the best workers there, but because I was on an agency, some cutbacks were being made. I was the first thing to go. I was devastated, I loved the job and got along well with everyone there. I told my driving instructor, she said "you jinxed it, didn't you?" Despite that, I didn't feel sorry for myself. Within three weeks, I had another job. A well-paid one this time, albeit not the most stable. But it was enough to resume the driving lessons.

I kept the momentum going, and had a date locked in for the Black Belt grading on March 26th. I would train at least five days a week, sometimes twice daily, if I could fit it in. I spent years learning the syllabus, up until this point. Little did I know a few months before you grade, you're handed another folder full of new moves and variants of the ones you already know. Not only that, but you also had to perfect them in three months. (In both stances) Have you ever tried throwing with your opposite hand? Well, now imagine throwing jump-spinning kicks above the head level in your unnatural stance. It was a lot to take in, I had to be at peak fitness, so I got myself into amazing condition. Until two weeks before grading day... I couldn't believe it; I had only gone and injured my back trying to do a jump-spinning back kick in reverse stance on the punchbag. I didn't fully rotate, it felt like I dislodged my right hip, and something in my lower spine clicked. I fell to the floor and was in quite a bit of pain. I was seriously concerned. I thought, please, not now. Not after all these months of painstaking training and dedication. I went indoors, took some painkillers, and hoped I'd wake up the next day as right as rain. That wasn't to be the case. I woke up with a sore back and felt like, at any moment, it was going to cease up and I'd crumble to the floor like dropped Lego.

I tried to remain optimistic as I still had two weeks to get better. I was starting to taper the training down a bit anyway. The bulk of the hard work was done. Another week of cardio would have been helpful though. But there was no point in worrying about it, I had to adapt and overcome the situation if possible. Leading up to the day, I was still in pain, it hadn't eased much, if at all. I was advised by those close to me to pull the grading and rebook it for another day. I refused point blank, and said no way! I knew it was my ego making that decision for me. I couldn't back out at the last minute. It would look like I bottled it! Rescheduling would also not have been easy. I got up on the morning of the grading feeling extremely nervous and a bit sore. Anna was excited to be able to say she was dating a Black Belt, but at the same time, she advised me not to do it if I was in serious pain. "Serious" pain to me is that you can't physically move and need stronger drugs than you can get over the counter. I wasn't 100% sure I would be able to pull off every move to perfection, but I was going to give it a damn good try. I was also toying with whether or not to tell Ross that I had hurt my back. I didn't want it to look like I was trying to get an easy ride, because I certainly wasn't. I wanted the same treatment as everybody else, no matter how brutal it was.

On the way there, I told him what I had done. His reply was, "Well, we're not going to go easy on you". I instantly regretted telling him and thought, why didn't I just keep that to myself? I knew it was true, and obviously, he thought I was trying it on.

110

Then, to make matters worse, we were talking away and discussing the stipulations for the grading. Ross had told me before, but reminded me that a Black Belt grading took an average of 9–10 hours to complete. For some, it stretched to 14 hours, and if you think there's a break for breakfast or lunch. No! No, there isn't. It's two or three minutes after each section; and each section could take hours. I'll be forever grateful to one of the senior black belts, Jerry, who gave me a solid bit of advice the week before. He said to take Lucozade tablets with me and that they will help get me through it, and they did. I was already overcome with nerves and anxiety. Whilst En-route to the destination, Ross dropped a bombshell of all bombshells. I had to perform a head-level snap kick after every block in the syllabus. There were over thirty blocks in the whole syllabus, and when you took into account that you had to do front and reverse kicks in both stances, with ten repetitions of every single technique, from red belt to brown belt and then the same through the ghost techniques. It equated to nearly 6,000 repetitions. That's before your Kata, also in both stances, eight rounds of semi-contact sparring against a fresh opponent every round, a tile break, then five rounds of full contact. Just when you thought that was bad, there was a seven-minute continuous round of ground fighting against two opponents at the same time. The idea was to break you mentally as well as physically. Just what I needed, aye.

Unfortunately for me, in round three of my full contact fight, I got clocked with a heavy shot to the ribs. I felt something crack, and I dropped to the floor. I got up on the nineth second of the ten count and held my gloves up to carry on. Ross said "you've got me next and you still have your ground fighting and your mind, body, and soul to do". I reiterated I didn't want to fail, and he said, "don't be stupid! You stepped up, got in there to fight, and proved that you were more than willing to do it. That's all we were looking for. You got further than most". I smiled and muttered, "Okay". Although still sceptical, we started the ground fighting. I was getting tapped out left, right, and center, as I was fighting two opponents at once. One of them was choking me out, whilst the other one was getting me in a leg or ankle lock. I didn't stand a chance. But I got through it, just about. You are probably wondering what the hell the mind, body, and soul is. Well... Basically, for the last four months, I was supposed to be practicing how to meditate. I didn't do it! I knew it was going to be a placebo at best. It takes years of diligent practice and dedication to master meditation. The test is; that you are to take a full-contact strike from your instructor and show no pain. It could be a punch to the arm, full-contact kick to the leg. Or something of that nature. Not the face, because that would be a little extreme. So, after the grading is complete, you are left to your own devices for about five minutes to center yourself and try to get into a higher state of mind. Before Ross left, he said, "imagine a cartoon and visualise you walking through woods and fields, and you can see your breath going in and out of your mouth". He then walked out, and as he did, he turned as I was getting up from the ground and said "No, stay there; it's fine. Relax and picture the scene". As hard as I tried, I couldn't get myself to that point, no matter what I did. It was at that exact moment that I thought, Fuck! Maybe I should have done the meditation practice for the last few months. But what was to come, would be my saving grace.

Something out of the ordinary happened! As I lay on my back, all broken, disheveled, and utterly battered after having the spirit beaten out of me for hours on end. Whilst waiting for the return of Ross. I then thought about my dad and brother and the fact that if they could see me now, how proud they'd be. I had my elbows on the floor, put my hands out, and visualised them both being on either side of me, holding one hand each. I gently closed my hands; I swear I felt their presence. I got to hold my dad's hand one last time. Emotional and still flooded with adrenaline, I told myself, you are nearly there. Let's get this done! I zoned out so much, I was close to falling asleep. Then I heard the door crack open. A single set of ominously slow footsteps walk into the room. It was unnerving, I immediately came too. Ross had explained to me that he would walk in alone, help me get to my feet and give me two or three minutes to relax myself while standing up, before he struck me. He grabbed both my hands, helped me up, and said, take a few minutes. He then began circling me to pick a spot to strike. He stopped. I took a deep breath and waited for the full-contact kick or punch. He moved on and walked around again. Then he stopped on the right side of me. I took a breath and prepared myself once more. He walked off again, towards the back of me. I knew it wouldn't be a strike from behind my back, so I relaxed. BOOM! An inside leg kick to the inner left thigh with his shin bone. I slid across the floor but didn't register the pain at all. I kept my eyes shut. Ross said, "open your eyes". I opened them to be met with Jack and Callum, barely two feet from me, looking straight into my eyes. I was so confused as to how they were there? Ross walked around to face me and grabbed me by the head, and said "you fucking did it. It's over. You passed!" I nearly cried from exhaustion and relief. He threw me a mars bar and a can of coke. And said "You may get emotional. You've just had 7 hours of hell, so let it out." Before he had finished that sentence, I had tears in my eyes. I didn't fully bawl them out, it was just pure relief!

I didn't have a clue as to the extent of my injuries until I got back to Anna's flat. My ribs were caved in on my right side. My whole torso was wonky. I had a sore head and a very sore back. Anna and I were supposed to be going out to celebrate. There was no chance of that, I was in absolute agony and could barely walk. A takeaway it was. Despite being in serious pain, I was over the moon that I passed my Black Belt grade. Not only that, but it was also my highest pass mark since I had been doing kickboxing. 94% and the fastest Black Belt grading ever in the club. Completing everything in just under 7 hours. All the hard work was worth it in the end. I had no idea how painful the next 18 months were going to be at that time. I went back to kickboxing a little under a month later, far too soon! There were certain techniques I couldn't throw due to the back injury. But I could still do the basics, even though it caused me pain. Halfway through the second lesson, I threw a hook kick off the front leg. I felt the strangest sensation run down my leg, from the top of my hip to my foot. It was like pins and needles. I tried stamping my foot on the ground to get rid of it, it wasn't budging for love nor money. A day later, I was barely able to move. That sensation turned out to be the start of severe sciatica that would last well over a year. To make matters worse, the job I had was cable-pulling. We were pulling huge industrial cables into a new hospital in its infancy stages. It was backbreaking work without being injured, never mind with injuries. I had to keep up with my driving lessons, which were painful in themselves. Regardless of what negative connotations came with my Black Belt, I kept on ploughing through.

As I was out of action physically, I decided to start recording some music and writing more songs. I was doing whatever I could to try and stay in a positive frame of mind. I was still going out on the weekends with Anna, albeit more often than not a nice restaurant rather than a pub. I had a decent wage packet every week for a change, so that was keeping my spirits up. Driving was coming along well, and I also took solace from the fact I was smashing through my yearly goals ahead of schedule. July comes, and there's now talk of doing my driving test. I'd already passed the theory a couple of months before, on the second attempt. I was feeling more than comfortable driving. We had a date locked in for August. I had one final lesson coming up before the test, and I drove like an absolute idiot! I couldn't get to grips with the three-lane roundabout, and I drove badly afterwards. The instructor said, "I don't think it's a good idea for you to go into a test off the back of a bad lesson. Let me see if I can rebook you in a different area". It turned out to be a blessing in disguise, as I avoided the dreaded roundabouts. September 1st was the new date. I had a few lessons to familiarise myself with the new area. I instantly felt much more comfortable. I had a great lesson before the test and then drove there. When we arrived at the test centre, it had the feeling of a dentist's waiting room. Except there was much more tension in the air. My test Examiner came out; I noticed another guy with him. I wondered what was going on. He said this is Andrew, He will be sitting in the back. Don't worry; he is just observing what I am doing, not you. Straight away, I thought shit! Now, I have two people watching me, and I can't even see what the other one is doing. I had to put it to the back of my mind and focus on the test. I had passed a harder test earlier in the year and always seemed to do well when the pressure was on. Halfway through, and I had drove really well; to the best of my knowledge. I then got asked to drive down this narrow road and do a three-point turn. As I looked behind me to reverse, I had completely forgotten that the other guy was behind me and jumped. They chuckled a bit. He was right when he said "you won't know I'm there". I got compliments on my clutch control and started the drive back. I had passed, thank God! I only got five minors. I was ecstatic!

I had finally turned my life around and done some positive things with my time and money! I was still struggling a lot upstairs and was still getting these waves of cold numbness that hit me daily. But I refused to sink or be beaten. I was fighting for my life this year, broken physically and even more mentally. I kept going, like nothing could halt my progress. So, I thought.

A couple of weeks later, I am working on the building site pulling cables in North London. All of a sudden, I couldn't see a thing. Everything started spinning, and I couldn't breathe. I go to the toilet and splash my face. I have no idea what the hell is going on, and I can't seem to shake it off. My supervisor walks in and asks if I am alright. I said, Barry, "I can't fucking see; I don't know what's going on". I took a knee and tried to gather myself. A first aider comes and grabs me and takes me into the offices next door. He asks me a few questions and gives me a bottle of water. He identifies it as a panic attack. I had never had one, so I didn't know what they were like, and my god, they are intense! I got sent home, and from that day on, I felt like it was later used against me, to not take me along to the next job. They wanted me gone! I was given some reassurance that wouldn't be the case by people around me, as they couldn't do that. They didn't sack me, but I noticed that I am being treated differently compared to other lads on the firm. Around the mid-October time. I am on the roof of the building, holding onto a heavy cable for dear life. My phone is ringing constantly; it won't stop! I thought this had to be my mum with something trivial, probably. I answered, and it was a guy named James. He said "Ronnie?" I replied "yes speaking". He then, in an aggressive tone, he says "I am from the Council; you owe us nearly £9,000!!!" I replied, "I don't know what you're talking about. I think you have the wrong guy". He sharply cut me down and said he hadn't. "We're currently sitting here with your mum. She tells us you haven't been paying her rent"! I disagree and say, "Look, mate, I don't know what you're talking about. But I have to go now, I am currently holding a massive cable on top of a building with my colleagues beneath me, it's too dangerous for me to talk right now". I put the phone down and thought, here we go again. Just when I was on a roll.

When I get home and ask my old girl what is going on? She then claims to back up what the council were saying, and said "you need to pay it, son. I don't have the money". A big row ensues, and I am still none the wiser as to what the hell has happened. I call my sister absolutely raging! She calmed me down and said, "don't worry, we'll get to the bottom of it". I explain that I have been putting money into Mum's account for years and can't understand it. I collated all my evidence in the form of bank statements and my sister and I booked an appointment to see James from The Council. I walk in with years' worth of statements proving I have been paying. To be fair to James, he held his hands up and said, sir, I am so sorry. It was such a convincing story your mum gave me. Although I was relieved, it then all of a sudden dawned on me that my mum had tried to frame me for fraud. I was livid and went back home to have it out with her. Tracey calmed it all down and asked her why? Mum said to her that your brother wasn't paying me enough. Despite Tracey's efforts to get through to mum she wouldn't accept her responsibility. She had been drinking all my rent money for five years since dad had died. Slowly getting further and further in arrears.

On the 28th of October, only two weeks later, I get laid off. What would have been my brother's birthday of all days? My great year had come to a shuddering halt. Unfortunately, it was only the start of the massive fall from grace. I was out of work right on top of Christmas again! Things at home were unrepairable between mum and myself. I wish I hadn't hung around, in all honesty. But I promised my dad I wouldn't abandon her once he'd passed. Mid November, my mum has a mental health nurse visit the house, as my sister said she had to get help and that we were going to step back. My mum did her usual and put on another flawless acting performance. She was saying I was neglectful and evil. She blamed me for my brother's suicide in front of the nurse, and that was the final straw I stormed out of the room. I was 12 years old when my brother killed himself. She turned around and said, "It was your fault your brother took his life. You wouldn't let him come back home." That sentence stuck with me. I never did forgive her for it.

Tracey came outside to calm me down and brought me back into the room just as the nurse hits upon something that touches a nerve with mum. I catch my mum's face changing. It was like she was two different people sometimes. Her eyes glazed over and went all dark. Her expression went from solemn and woe is me, to this vehemently nasty stare. The nurse immediately jotted down some notes in her book, a week later, mum was admitted to a mental health facility. While she was away, despite all these hurdles in my way, I tried my best to get on top of things.

Anna suggested working at a school so we could share the summer holidays. I got my head down and started looking hard for work, updated my CV, and put some serious hours into applying for jobs. Out of the blue, I got an interview for a pastoral worker at a local school on the 6th of December. I was buzzing and couldn't believe I landed an interview for a role I had never done before. It was the only way to bounce back. I couldn't afford to sink after such a positive year. I had put in far too much groundwork; to let it all go down the pan now. I had never prepared for an interview before. You never know what curve balls they will throw at you. Doing door-to-door taught me to think on my feet and adapt to situations as they unfold. So, I patiently waited a week for the interview and did my best to stay focused. But nothing could prepare me for the cascade of events that were to come.

Chapter 12

The Breaking Point

It's 6th of December, the day of the interview. I was understandably nervous. With all the unnecessary drama with my mum going on in the background, it was hard to keep my head on straight. Regardless, I got myself suited and booted and walked out the door. Armed with little confidence and a handful of optimism. As soon as I stepped out of the porchway, I was faced with three people, two women and one gentleman. I had just under half an hour to get to my destination; it was a quarter-hour drive, so time was of the essence. The people at the door were from the mental health facility my mum was in. They were requesting her keys to the house. I explained that I was in a rush and trying to get to an interview. After they presented me with I.D. I ran into the house to grab her purse and said, "If they're not in there, then I have no clue where they could be. I haven't got time to look around right now, I'm so sorry!" They were nice and pleasant. It was an unfortunately, timed arrival. One of the nurses said mum would be due back home on Thursday. She said, "If we can't find the house keys today, they'll change the locks in a few days and give you a new set." I replied, "That's fine, thank you", and dashed off. It was the last thing I needed right before an interview. I got there ten minutes early, despite my unsolicited visitors. The interview was so intense; there were three of them all asking questions; I felt surrounded! I got through it quite well and only stumbled on one question, which was one of those weird ones that was completely unrelated to the actual job.

As soon as I got out of there, I called Anna and told her how it all went. I was quite hopeful of getting through to the next stage for a second interview. The bounce-back was on. I arrive home feeling reinvigorated, walk up my path, put the key in the door, turn it. It doesn't move! I can't get in. They'd changed the locks while I was at my interview. Despite promising they wouldn't do so until Thursday. I was effectively stuck outside, with my dog and my cat locked inside. I tried every lock, none of my keys were working. I immediately got angry! I called my sister; she didn't answer! I rang Anna, and she didn't answer either but called me back two minutes later. I was seething with unfiltered rage! She said, "Don't do anything stupid; think about things logically". That was good advice. However, I was trying to rip a brick out of the wall to smash a window. I was angrier about them locking my animals in than anything else. The reality of the situation hadn't hit me yet. I walked up to the back door and gave it a little kick, contemplating whether to put it through. Then, I tried a three-quarter power kick on the front door and smashed the panel off. It flew through the porch-way and hit the back door on the other side. I stepped through the middle of the door and thought to myself, well, I have come this far. I might as well rip the other door down. I did exactly that. I am then frantically ringing around to try and find somewhere for Max and Avi to go and stay until I get something sorted. Luckily, Rhian's mum was willing to take Avi, and my friend Phil up the road had offered to look after Max for a little while.

The red mist had fully descended, and I was in no mood for anyone or anything at that moment. I grabbed Avi, put her in a cat carrier and locked Max in my room to stop him from escaping, as I had rendered the doors completely useless. I put Avi in the car and drove her to Longfield. Only fifteen minutes down the road. On the way there, my phone rang; it was a number I didn't recognise. A nurse from the hospital. She happily proceeded to inform me that they had changed the locks on my house and that my mum had issued the request. It sounded like she was extremely gleeful about this and spoke in the most condescending tone I have ever witnessed in my entire life. Unfortunately, this sent me off the cliff edge. I screamed down the phone at her, calling her all the names under the sun and letting her have it. Ultimately, proving my mum right about the things she had been saying about me while under their care. She's lucky because if it weren't for my sister, I'd have been in that

119

hospital, gunning for her and everyone involved. I had only been driving for a few months, my car was swaying all over the road, where I was in a state of complete indignation shouting at that nurse. The nurse took pleasure in making me homeless and did not even consider my situation or how I have tried to rebuild my life. She ended up putting the phone down on me. I would have handled that situation differently today. If only I had the head on my shoulders, then, that I have now. Hindsight is a wonderful thing.

Tracey called me back as I was on my way to rehome Avi. I was inaudible and incoherent when she answered, shouting swear words, and that was how I was going to go up to that hospital to smash the place up. I had tipped over the edge, and there was no coming back. I have always had a vicious temper. Luckily, these days, I am much more thoughtful and calmer in the face of adversity. I was watching my life crumble before my eyes for the umpteenth time, and the snowball had only just started rolling downhill. Tracey managed to stop me from going to the hospital, as there is absolutely no doubt I would have been arrested. I dropped the cat off with Rhian's mum and then made my way back to the house. When I got back 'home', Tracey met me. She said, "Right, you're homeless, you better get all your stuff out." The realisation that I had nowhere to live hit me. I knew I wouldn't be on the streets, but it was still a huge thing to deal with right before Christmas. I was so close to throwing the towel in. We spent ages moving all my stuff out, to Tracey's garage. Within two hours, I had an interview. I'd lost my home, my dog, and my cat. All the good things I managed to achieve in 2016 went straight out of the window.

I stayed at Anna's, and my sister had me round for tea a couple of times a week. I was desperately hanging on at this point. Unbelievably, a week later, I got a call for the second interview. Most people would have just said, sorry, life circumstances have unfortunately made me unavailable. I didn't though. I gritted my teeth like an idiot and proceeded to pursue a change of career. When I should have put my mental health first! I went along to the second interview because I was almost to the point of not giving a toss about what happened to me. I think that came out as confidence to the people holding the interview. I left there knowing in the back of my mind, outside of that room, my life was a total fucking mess, and these people had no clue! I wanted the job, but bigger things were occurring in my private life. I honestly didn't know where to start. Everything was just a loop of misery. I had still not spoken to my mum. She was trying to contact me, to get something I had taken from the house; I did it to prove a point. I took a photo she had of my dad. Is that cruel? Yeah, it probably was, but so is being framed for fraud and being made homeless, telling everyone your son was an abuser, and trying to put my pets into Battersea without my consent. One of the reasons I got Max was to keep her company when I wasn't there, as she was lonely without Dad. I honestly never felt so useless in my entire existence. Anna had just moved house, so she had loads going on herself. I was on deck to help out there I suppose, so that's what I did. If anything, it came as a welcome distraction.

The following Monday, I'm decorating Anna's house to help out whilst I wasn't working. My phone rings. It's the school. I had given up on it to be quite honest; then they offered me the job. I was due to start in the new year. I didn't want to work in a school, but the benefit of being off for so long in the holidays was useful. It also saved any more arguments between Anna and me. I made another terrible decision and took the job. I was so disinterested in life again. I started the year so well and fought back from the depths of despair, despite having to basic start from square one again.

I started the new role at the school, begrudgingly. Not that I had a choice. Work was work, and it's not like I had loads of options on the table. I was also teaching kickboxing at the weekends, as Ross was no longer available. That was ok, because at least I enjoyed it, and it gave me a much-needed outlet. Although the lessons were shocking, I just let people mess about in them. I was there, but I wasn't. 28th January 2017, whilst I was half-way through teaching a lesson I get a call from Tracey. She sounded peculiar and asked where I was. I reply that I am teaching a kickboxing lesson. She says, "Oh... OK, don't worry then; I'll call you back in a bit. What time do you finish?" I replied, "no, come on. What's wrong?" She said "I can't tell you now, darling. Who are you with? Is Anna with you?" I said "no, just bloody tell me. What's going on?" In a fractured and distant tone, she replied, "Mum's dead". I sit down on a step outside the room in shock. I say, "Fucking hell, how?" Tracey replies that she was found unresponsive on the kitchen floor in a pool of blood. I immediately circle back to the time my dad said to her, you're going to end up like your mother if you carry on like this. Ironically, that is exactly how her mum was found. I can't explain the feelings I felt at that moment. I didn't cry; I didn't register. I was just shocked! I went back into the lesson and explained to the next highest grade that my mum had just died and asked if he could he take over. With only half of the lesson left, he was happy to oblige. I walked out of there completely despondent. I called Anna and told her. She was also shocked and said to be careful driving and get myself to see Tracey as soon as you can. When I arrived at my sisters, we were both numb and lost for words. When a parent dies that you didn't get on with, there's a range of emotions that can't be explained. No matter what she will always be first and foremost my mum despite how she treated me. I felt the pain of losing her but there was a strange deep-seated numbness that holds the trauma from her actions.

It's mid-February 2017. My mum's funeral is taking place. Less than ten people are present. It was sad to see, but that tells the story itself. Alcohol will segregate you from everyone in life, and in death. Anna came along to support me, but I was more concerned about it bringing back bad memories for her than worrying about myself. It was a strange occasion for me. I found it hard to cry. That may sound alien to most of you reading this book, but the amount of stuff she put me through was tough to bear. I was no angel either; we had lost our relationship the day my brother committed suicide. I sat there sombre, and I won't lie, a wave of relief hit me at one point. Mum was miserable for years and said multiple times she wanted to die. Unfortunately, she spent years trying to do it with alcohol; and eventually got what she wanted. My sister was a little more upset than me, as she had more time with mum years before what happened. The thing that haunted me until very recently was the fact that she died, and we weren't even on talking terms. There's no coming back from that. It's something I have to live with. I ended up getting closure eventually, as you'll find out later.

The last four months, my life had been flipped upside down. I still needed to sort out the minor issue of being homeless. I had been in and out of the council offices trying to get a flat. They were refusing to help me, saying I wasn't on the previous tenancy and that I wasn't a priority. Tracey, once again, was my saviour. She managed to get me another meeting with someone in a different department to see if I was eligible for more help. This lady was brilliant and made all the difference in me getting a place. I was on my last legs and on the verge of tears in this meeting. The lady threw me a lifeline and said, "Look, I can see how desperate you are and how much you need this. Off the record, don't say you're homeless. Say you are sofa surfing." Tracey and I looked bewildered. She said, "I know that sounds unbelievable. But if you are sofa surfing, then you are other people's problem. If you can get a few good friends to vouch for you and say you're an inconvenience, then you'll be much more likely to get a place." Armed with this new intelligence, we approached the Council one more time. Halfway through the meeting, my sister played an ace card I didn't know she was holding and said, "You know what my brother has been through, it wouldn't look good if he did something stupid when you could have helped him." The two people holding the meeting, one being James, who wrongly accused me of fraud, previously, nervously gazed over at his colleague. They changed their tact sharply. I was sitting there, a broken man. They could see I was a shell at best. It had already been four months; I had all but given up hope. They then agreed to put me on the list and make me a Band-A. Which is high priority. I checked their website daily to find a flat and bid on it. After a couple more months passed, I found one. Unfortunately, mentally, I had already paid the price. Which would lead to more unrest between me and the ones around me.

It came as no shock, that two weeks later, Anna and I split up. I couldn't deal with the pressure of having three step-kids. I then got fired from the school. They didn't know what I was going through outside of work and I couldn't be bothered to explain. These people weren't on my level from the get-go. I strongly disagreed with how the school was run and the way they labelled kids. I am escorted off the premises for some reason. Now, this has to be some sort of record - from the door of the school to the door of my car, I have another job. I rang an old work colleague, and within two days I was back knocking doors. It wasn't ideal by any means. But it's better than being jobless. I adopted this false mindset and hit the ground running. I was calling in with ten leads, just in the morning some days. Hitting crazy sales return numbers, my new bosses were like, who is this guy? I set a new standard and was flying. I made friends with a girl called Monica, she offered that level of understanding and empathy I wasn't getting elsewhere. A soul buddy of sorts, if you will. It made me notice what my previous relationship was lacking and what I wanted. Albeit not Monica herself! There was only so long before my fake confidence and a great new friend could get me through.

Within a couple of months, whilst also in the transition of being homeless and getting my flat, trying to hit high numbers on a commission-based job. Going through several bouts of physiotherapy and acupuncture to fix my injuries, the inevitable happens. I have a major breakdown! I was rushed to the hospital immediately. I had finally snapped. I couldn't stop crying. I was shaking from head to foot. Tracey came around to rush me in to get professional help. I was on the verge of visiting my brother once again. I simply couldn't take much more of life. Scott also showed up, I have never seen him look as worried or concerned as he did that day. Scott is not the kind of guy who gets phased by much. I'll never forget the look on his face. Even he couldn't believe the state of me. Despite him being a hard-nosed, unsympathetic twat the majority of the time, he's also the realest guy I know and has a heart of gold. I saw a nurse, they put me on anti-depressants and recommended that I get counselling as soon as I could. I got put in touch with Mind and started the process right away. My poor sister probably thought, oh no, not again. I go home to my new flat, although I am so grateful and relieved, I am feeling so lonely and desperate to find peace. I decided I couldn't find that in life. I was still getting these waves of ice-cold numbness that hit me almost hourly. I was done! I spent all this time fighting for justice and my flat, but it was too little too late.

I went to my kickboxing bag and grabbed my black belt. I walked up to my pull-up bar above my doorway, tied a solid knot, and made a noose. I told myself there wouldn't be any mistakes this time around. I don't even use a platform to put my feet on. I'm so intent on ending my life that I simply start to hang from the belt while almost in a seated position with my heels on the floor. I can feel the blood rushing to my head. Blackness shrouds me, and I start to fade out. Then, a bright white light appears in the distance. I can feel myself slipping away! As the light gets closer and closer, the overwhelming feeling of peace and serenity hugs me closely. That moment was beautiful! My pain left me, and I felt free—free of agony, free of misery, free of whatever this was. Then, just before the lights shut off, I see my sister's face standing over my grave. I see myself as a little boy chucking that black rose onto my brother's coffin. I see all my friends crying and the pain I left behind. I reach up with my last bit of strength. I grab the belt and save myself. When they say your life flashes before your eyes before you die, well, I can confirm this is true! I get to my knees, gasping for air, and undo the belt from my now red, blotchy neck. I burst out crying, and half an hour later. I called my sister. I admit to Tracey that I had gotten close to taking my life. She doesn't know these details in full, and I'm sorry, sis, that you have to read this here. It won't happen again, I promise! The hospital realised how seriously I needed help. They put me in touch with the crisis team. I'm on suicide watch for the next two months and am monitored a few times a week. Tracey tried to be present as much as possible when they visited. I was asked various questions about my mental state and if I was having dark thoughts. They did a great job of helping me turn the corner and get back on my feet. I was hurting, but as the weeks rolled by, I became less suicidal and gradually saw a little hope in life again.

I couldn't function alone and got back with Anna. I knew deep down that wasn't the answer, but I was just so lost.

As the year fizzles out, I am slowly starting to get my head back together. I was determined to pick myself back up and hit 2018 hard. I decided the only way to achieve this was by adopting the mindset I had in 2016 and writing a list! So, here we go again. Making one more attempt at this thing we call life. It was time to dust myself down and start over. I was in familiar territory, jobless and at the start line again. I started researching Calisthenics to get fit, as the pain was easing after treatment. I estimated, I was about two months away from making a start. Weirdly, I have an eerily similar beginning to the year as I did in 2016. I got an interview for another job at a school. The role is for a D.T. Technician. This was hilarious! For a multitude of reasons. The main reason, is the fact I can't build a fucking Wendy House, never mind help students build complex designs for GCSEs. I arrived very apprehensive and nervous, as I had no clue what I was doing. Even when I did my GCSE in Design Technology, someone else built most of my project for me.

I meet the head of the department, and we exchange some niceties. He then handed me a folder. "Please go through that folder Ronnie, and just write the names of all the machinery. Refrain from using the internet to Google the answers. I'll be back soon". I skimmed through this folder. I did not have a clue what three-quarters of the machines were. Well, this is a great start; I've not even got to the interview stage and I haven't got the job. So much for getting a break, I thought, oh well. I'll just have to be honest and say I don't know, accept my humble pie, and be on my way. Then, in a strange turn of events, it was almost like the universe heard me. The fire alarm went off. The head of the department came out and said "you may as well stay there. It's only a drill; there's no point in you coming out". I smiled with glee and googled my heart out. I named every single machine bar one. I said I just went blank. When they told me, I recoiled in my seat, snapped my fingers, and said, oh, of course, and laughed. Sales had stood me in good stead. I somehow got through the interview, but towards the end, I thought I may have overdone the bullshitting. I got a few sly looks. They shake my hand, and on I go, not expecting much from it, if I'm being honest.

The following afternoon my phone rings, and the school offer me the job. I am gob smacked! I politely accept the job and quickly find myself, that Friday being shown around the school. The head of department shows me the workshop I would be working in, and it is a total mess. He says it may take me months to sort it all out. My eyes lit up! He then takes me upstairs to the art department, where the two other rooms were, that needed serious attention. That was another few weeks' work at least. I really didn't want to be there, and there were few things that I could think of worse than working with teenagers. But at least this gave me some time to avoid the inevitable situation and figure out what I wanted to do.

I am basking in the fact that I am being left alone and allowed to potter around in my workshop. Even the kids weren't allowed in there, as it was a health and safety issue. (Perfect!) I was in my element. Then, the head of the tech department asked for proof of my GCSE results. I explained that I had been homeless and that all my stuff was in boxes in various locations. It was a complete lie. I knew exactly where they were. But I couldn't hand them over and get myself sacked. He was very understanding and said not to worry, just bring them as and when you get your hands on them. I'd bought myself another couple of weeks, at least. I still hadn't made a dent in the workshop, so I knew I could blag that for another two months at least. The teacher who was head of the year wasn't quite as convinced of me, though. I knew it was a matter of time before he was onto me.

Another month flies by, and I am starting to make headway with the workshop. I have now resorted to labelling drawers and sharpening tools, sometimes the same one twice, to kill time. Every time someone came in, I'd pretend to be busy. They kindly gave me a laptop to do research on. I don't think they meant research calisthenics, workout plans, sports science, and nutrition. I learned so much stuff in the next few months. It just wasn't what they expected! I couldn't use the workshop clean-up as an excuse any longer. I had to move to the other rooms, and unbeknownst to me, they needed me to come in for a few days of the summer holidays to clean up the other rooms upstairs. My plans dwindled, and the pressure was on. They approached me for my GCSE results once again. I said they were in my sister's garage, that had leaked and destroyed a lot of my belongings. "As soon as she gets it fixed, I'll try to dig them out and hope they're not damaged". I could see he started getting suspicious at this stage and gave me a look of disbelief. As if to say, I think you might be bullshitting me now. It was written all over his face. I mean, me? Come on now... Realistically, I knew I had about a month left before I was exposed. So, I got to work and started applying for another job. I couldn't keep this up for much longer. I was struggling financially which was taking its toll on my relationship again, amongst many other things. Plus, I couldn't get the sack from another job. I managed to land four interviews for various other jobs, mostly caretaker roles.

I get an email to come in for an interview. It looks like I had a way out after all. I am optimistic about this role, as it's £6,000 more than I was on, and even that wasn't much to write home about. Then it seemed by divine intervention that, on the day of the first interview, I couldn't find the school. It didn't look like it even existed. I searched on Google Maps. I drove around for ages looking for this place and couldn't find it for the life of me. I drove away dejected. and thought, well, that's me screwed! Out of all the jobs I had lined up, this was the one I actually wanted. A week later, one of the other schools called regarding their vacancy. They wanted me to come in as soon as I could. I jump at the chance, as it is on my doorstep. I get a great vibe as soon as I walk through the door. The guy I met for the job was a proper old-school bloke. Really down to earth. I was so hopeful when I left. I said to Anna, "I'd be shocked if I didn't get that one". Things between us weren't great again. She was getting fed up with me being skint, and not holding down a job. Which I understood. It was just due to what had gone on. We were arguing far too much and it became a very unhealthy environment for not just us, but her kids. We split up again! It just wasn't meant to be. We kept going around in circles to no avail.

I went to The Winchester to see all my friends who worked in the pub and waited for it to all blow over. It wasn't to drink; it was to socialise. I couldn't bear being alone at the time. It was my place of refuge for a few months. None of them understood how much they helped me without directly helping me. So, a shoutout to you guys. I would have been lost without you. Whilst I was alone, I am still putting in some serious training outside of work; I threw myself into it to keep my mind busy. I couldn't train all the time and going back to a flat with no one in it was tough. I went from a hustle-and-bustle house with three kids, a dog, and a cat to absolute stillness. I needed something to keep my brain busy as well. I decided to run my own Hip Hop based Twitter page. This was where I met Homegrown L. Lauren, as I now know her. She killed me with kindness one day with a reply to a comment I left on a musician's post. I found it so epic that I couldn't do anything but respond in a manner that admitted it. Well, we still talk to this day via text, mainly because she lives over 210 miles away. We're Hip-Hop buddies, the modern-day version of pen pals. We have only met once, and that was at the tail end of the "pandemic." We hit it off and can go six months without talking, pop up, say hello, then disappear again. Lauren helped me through some darker times without really realising it. Our journeys are almost parallel in the fact that we both have had issues in the past with substances and being on the wrong path. Today, we're both on a positive path and living a healthy lifestyle. She's a diamond, and I'm so proud to see her turn her life around as well. At the specific time we started talking, I was struggling quite badly. It was good timing, and obviously, for a reason. I felt it was only right to shout her out in this book. At the time, things were a bit morbid. I felt secluded. I didn't do well in the quiet. It ate me up. Having someone to talk about stuff, who shared the same passion made a massive difference! It was nice to have that mental outlet, but I was still quite an angry young man deep down. I needed to address it before I fell back into that hot-tempered version of me. I and no one else liked.

So, I hit the gym hard! One particular day, I decided to go on the punchbag. It had been a while. I needed to get some deep-seated anger out of me before I exploded. I can feel this guy watching me from over my shoulder. It's making me feel a bit uneasy. Does he think I'm shit? Is he judging me? Then I think, Fuck him. Just crack on with what you're doing and stop caring! So, I ignored him. Then I get a tap on my shoulder. "You alright, mate. I'm John". It's the guy who was watching me. I take a glove off and shake his hand. I didn't know at that moment; my whole life was just about to change. He asked me, "How long have you been boxing, mate? "I stated I was a kickboxer, he praised me and said I looked decent on the bag. We had a good chat; he said he knew some fighters and he trained with them. I initially thought he was talking crap, but then he showed me photos of him on the doors with one of them because, around that time, he was thinking of quitting boxing and working security. Thank God he didn't as he went on to fight a well-known Mexican and make millions! I was shocked and started asking a few questions. He gave me his number and said to go down to the gym, where they train sometimes. I thought it was an interesting interaction and decided to take him up on his offer the following week. Unfortunately, because of my work commitments, I only had one day I could make it. We did some sparring and bag work. He then asked me what I did for work. I said I was working in a school and I'm on my backside financially. John said "my best mate needs someone at his place. It's a security role". I laughed and said, "Look at the size of me!" John said, "Don't be silly. You're handy enough. I'm no bigger than you and I work doors. Think about it. It's not bad money". I shook his hand and thanked him. I told him I'd get back to him in a few days.

I went away and did my research. I needed to make some big changes if I were to go down this route. I needed an S.I.A. badge, I needed to go on a course, and not only that, I had to get a new car to get me to work without risking my life, as the one I had turned itself off every time I changed down to second gear. There was so much to contemplate. The school started closing in on me. They kept on pestering me for my GCSE results. They also noticed my lack of presence and workload. The job I was certain of getting at the other school never called me back. The others I had lined up weren't great money. It was all chips on black. I said to myself, sod it! I texted John and said, "sign me up". I let him know I needed a badge and a course. He told me "It's fine; the job is yours. It's only August. They need you before Christmas, and you'll probably be in by September". I handed in my resignation to the school. I reckon I had a couple of weeks before they sacked me anyway.

The next thing you know I'm in North London doing a course. I was 34 years old and going nowhere! No career, bouncing from one job to another aimlessly. Thinking about this now, would I even be here if he hadn't spotted me that day and tapped me on the shoulder? Who knows where I would have ended up? I owe that man a beer someday. A classic example of right place, right time. It's one day into the course, and I am enjoying it. Most of the locks and holds I already knew from my kickboxing experience. The rest was common sense. Lunchtime comes, and I am sitting there, minding my own business. The only lady on the course walks in, and I catch her eye briefly. She smiles at me, approaches my table, and asks if she can sit there. I smiled and said, "Sure!" If I knew where this was going to end up, I would have said fuck no! We hit it off and began a decent conversation. Her name was Marta, a Polish lady. She seemed nice and normal. One of the rare times I massively misjudged someone.

The positive was, I found myself breezing through the course and picking things up relatively quickly. There was a written test and a practical test on the S.I.A. I passed the physical side of it with relative ease, and the test paper wasn't rocket science either. All I had to do was sit tight for a few days and await my results. I was quietly confident, as it's common sense. I find myself in a pub garden afterwards with Marta. She said "you have to come out and have a proper drink with me one day". Whilst her hand rubbing my inside thigh. She wasn't shy! Then she apologised for being forward. I laughed it off and agreed to meet her one day in the near future. (Mistake!) I was single and thought, why not have a bit of "fun?" As a few more drinks went down, we discussed meeting up a little more in-depth. She boldly turned around and said, "I want to put you on this table right now. I want you!" I blushed and laughed, but she wasn't playing any games and was deadly serious. Marta and I exchange numbers at the train station. Without warning, she lunges at me and shoves her tongue down my throat quite aggressively. I should have seen the writing on the wall then. I go to the "Winchester" and tell all my friends that I have pulled a frisky 45-year-old Polish woman and I am going to meet her this coming Saturday. I'm giving it the large one in the pub, my friends are all goading me and saying, "How do you find yourself in such weird situations? Only you could go on a security course, and something like this would happen."

Saturday arrives and I find myself on the drive to Heathrow with a slightly cautious feeling in my gut. As I turn up, I immediately feel a bit off. I already regret my impulsive single-man decision. I had never done this sort of thing before, I bet you're all thinking, course you haven't! Honestly, I never have, and I never will again! Marta opens the door. She already has an alcoholic drink in her hand and appears a little half-cut. Less than ten minutes pass. My trousers are around my ankles. I'm not going into details, but she's a bit shorter than she was when she answered the door. It was a long night. A long, loud, and painful night. The next morning, I couldn't wait to get out of there and made excuses. I was relieved to wake up with all my organs to be perfectly honest.
Marta was not keen to let me go, and kept trying to start a new conversation or offer me food. Then she said, "I have the feeling you want to leave". I said "no, it's just that traffic, it gets quite bad around my area and I have a long drive home". I get out at 11 a.m. Only to be met with a gaggle of her neighbours looking at me in disgust! I sheepishly cross the road looking at my car, worrying that the piece of shit wouldn't start. I am not religious, but I prayed that car was going to start. It did!!! I waved goodbye, drove off, and didn't look back. All I took away were blood scratches, a bruised pelvic bone, destroyed testicles, and bruises on my rib cage that lasted over a month. When I walked into the pub, they all burst out laughing and said, "Oh yeah, didn't go to plan then"? Let's just say, she was happier than me! Whilst I was

132

having a pint and telling the horror story, she texted me over ten times. I opened one of them. I had to press [read more] four times. The messages were honestly disturbing. Something about how I pierced her soul like an ice pick, and how she wanted me so hard she wanted to eat my heart, and how she'd fallen in love with me after our night together! Then she proceeded to send me about seven or eight YouTube videos, all of which were love songs. Everyone said run!!! But I didn't want to be an arsehole. I thought we were just having fun and even sold as such from the off. She had other plans. I replied and kept it sweet, although not misleading in any way. I woke up the next day with 21 unread messages. (ALL FROM HER) I replied a few times. I was trying to calmly mediate the situation. But she wasn't getting it. She came on stronger! Well, I blocked her in the end for my sanity and safety. She then hunted me down on Facebook Messenger, I blocked her on there too. She was going off on one; I didn't reply. If I were still suicidal, then things may have been different!

After this mentally traumatising event, I finally escaped my stalker! I turned my focus back to my potential new job. I sat tight for my results and waited with bated breath for my new SIA license to come through the post. I got the good news sooner than expected. I passed the course. S.I.A. contacted me and said I was clear to work. All I had to do was provide 5 years' work history for my new company, so that I could get through the vetting process. That proved nearly impossible, I was still waiting until December. In the end, I sent a nasty email to one of my old bosses, who was a friend of my dads from years ago. Who finally sent the details I needed to proceed. In between my ongoing dispute with my previous employer, My S.I.A. badge comes through the door. I hurriedly opened it and could not believe what I saw. I took the course way back in August and got confirmation of a pass by early September. So, the date they put on the card could have been any date from then on, right? Well, the expiration date on my card was October 28th. The date I got laid off from the job who wouldn't give me a reference, and more notably, my brother's birthday. I don't think I have to reiterate how mind-blowing that is. I looked up to the skies one more time and said, Cheers, Dave, we got there in the end, bruv. With tears of relief in my eyes. December 22nd, 2018. I started my new job. I was in a much better place mentally, and luckily, I had fully healed from all my beatings from kickboxing and Marta.

Surprisingly, I was looking for another Martial Arts club to join. I am toying with the notion of doing something weapons-based, as I'd be working in the city. Let's face it, knife crime is rife, and no one fights fair anymore. I was also looking into Muay Thai and other martial arts; what sealed the deal for me, was a show I came across on Netflix called Fight world. There were six episodes, I saw the Krav Maga one and skipped straight to it. After watching it, I filled out forms for the best Krav Maga club that seemed to be in my local area. There was a slight issue. Guess who was there? Yep, you guessed it, Anna. We wound up back in the toxic whirlpool of a relationship we both seemed to crave for some reason?!?! Right in the midst of my new job and terrible decision-making regarding women. A major event was about to take place.

I had been invited to Jack and Selina's wedding. They had chosen the date 26th of July my birthday! I will never let them live it down; how much they ruined the one day I get a year that is no longer about me. Cheers guys. Don't worry. We'll do what you want to do every year. I am joking. All banter aside, I love the pair of muppets. They're a great couple, and to be honest, they made a huge effort for me that day. I had a balloon tied to my chair and decorations all over my table. They'd put notes on other tables to get the rest of the guests to come and wish me a happy birthday. There were little number 35s all over my placemat. It was a nice touch; I must admit. I thought that would be it, until I had a gut feeling after Jack said the last words of his speech. "There is just one more thing. You know today is meant to be about us. Well, there's always one person who tries to make it about themselves". He glares at me through the crowd of 80 guests. A bit of me died inside; I was also quite pissed! He proceeds to say: Well, it's someone's birthday today, and they all stare at me. I jump up on my seat and raise my arms in the air to the whole venue. I didn't think it through. I knew just over half of the guests. They were the only half of the audience laughing.

No one else knew me and probably thought, What a twat! Then, much to my despair, Jack says, "Come and collect your card, mate." I died a little more inside and cautiously tread the long weaving journey to the front. Whilst instantly regretting my newfound bravery from about 30 seconds ago, I collect my card and try to walk off, he says, "oh no. Open it here, mate". Everyone jeered, so I had to. As soon as I opened it, which, by the way, was the biggest card I had ever seen in my life. There were pictures of me naked all over it, and others showing me dressed up in questionable attire. My now-famous sister impression was front and center. It was so embarrassing! Luckily, not many people saw the goods. I walked back with the card held tight to my chest, with people trying to grab it off of me. It was a good laugh and a memorable day to say the least. In the lead-up, those guys were going through some stuff as well. They entrusted me with some personal information that was quite upsetting and detrimental to their day. So, the fact that they even bothered with all that is a testament to who they are as people. So, despite forever casting a dark cloud over my birthday, thank you, guys, I suppose!

This day caused a lot more arguments between Anna and I, as she wasn't invited and got the hump. We weren't together when I got the invite, so what could I do? Oh guys, set another seat out for your already planned and paid-for wedding? Once the dust had settled, we moved past that, but still managed to fall back into the same old habits as we beforehand. None of us had a clue what 2020 would have in store for us. Like many others. The "pandemic," ruined a lot of businesses, sadly Krav Maga, became another casualty. We were then homebound. I missed training and the people, because it answered what was missing from my life at that particular point. I loved Krav. I was offered by the club instructor to go on an intense course to become an instructor myself and start my own club. Something that I didn't see coming. For some reason, Anna wasn't happy about that and was angry that I seemed to have waltzed in and gotten the limelight. It's not like I planned to, I was hoping deep down that she would be happy for me. But that wasn't to be. It never came to fruition anyway, unfortunately, being on the brink of 2020. But there was something I took away from the club that proved to be more important than any class, job offer, or Anna herself! She wasn't the only person I bumped into while training there. Whether that person would be for a short time or a lifetime. I was unsure?

Chapter 13

The Turning Point

You may have noticed I alluded to "The Advocate " earlier in the book. You probably thought, "Who the hell is that?" Well, I'm going to explain. I suppose I should clear up the nickname first, to stop you from wondering. It's a joke between her and I. She knows who she is, I don't need to name her, and for privacy; I want to keep it that way. Only my sister would be able to work it out.

So, I met "The Advocate" at... let's call it "Fight Club " in (2019), and we all know the first rule about... Yeah anyway! It was a daunting day for me. At the time my mental health was less than great; I hadn't been in that arena for a while because of the injuries I sustained from kickboxing. As soon as I walked through the door, about 15 guys turned around and stared at me. You know, like when you walk into that pub for the first time, and you're not from the village kind of way. I notice a lady in a wheelchair, at the back of the room. She was in one of those beep-beep, woop-woop-swish electric ones. I'll be transparent here. The first thing that popped into my brain was, wow, this club is hardcore. Then, I briefly looked around to take in my surroundings. I turned my back for only a few seconds, suddenly, she was standing next to me, I jolted a bit, like, what the fuck? Then, straight away, I thought, you still got it me ole son. This woman just performed a miracle to come and say hello to you. Next, she's going to turn my bottle of water into wine. I still remember the first words out of her mouth. I quote, "You got a skinhead and tattoos. You're going to fit in here. What kind of music do you like?" Straight away, I was like, she's amazing. She asked me what music I like. That's one of my first questions when I meet someone new. I replied. "Hip Hop mainly," she was like. "Ah, if you'd said rock and metal, you would have had all three." I said, "I am partial to some metal". I noticed she had a beaming smile and lovely energy. At that point, honestly, I thought, You're different! (Other than performing miracles, of course). I had no idea how important she would become to my journey.

"The Advocate" is a kind soul. She's had so much to deal with in her life and refuses to be beaten or give up. Our lives have been similar, we've both suffered trauma and pain along the way. When we got to know each other, we unloaded everything. Kindred spirits, some may say. I could go on this long rant about how many things we have in common, from the same star signs, to views, to getting the same outcomes on online tests. Such as both being Advocates, which, less than 5% of people are. Hence the nickname. I could never get used to the phenomenon that when we didn't talk for a few days and reconnected, all the same things had happened to us, or we'd been looking into the same subject. It's unexplainable and a bit weird, to be honest with you. I've never had that level of understanding with anyone else. We are always there for each other, whenever! Especially where mental health is concerned, and I know it's popular these days, but we were fucked up before it was cool! She is my go-to, and I am hers. I have many great friends and a lovely sister, as you know. But you either understand that level of darkness or you don't! Unless you have been down to that doldrum of nothingness, then you can't fully relate. We talk for up to three hours on the phone some days. Most of the time, laughing and joking. To outsiders, you may be thinking, well, if you've both got mental health issues, does one drag the other into a bad place? It's never happened once, at least not from my side. It is anything but that. "The Advocate" really changed my outlook on life. I'm not sure words alone can do it justice, but I'll try to explain.

When I was struggling a bit, she reached out and said, "Have you thought about hypnotherapy?" I said "no, not in the slightest". I was very suspicious about that sort of thing; never in a month of Sundays would it have crossed my mind. I had previously tried counselling; it wasn't for me. Although, it helped uncover one or two things, I never found it to have any significant impact. After a little bit of deliberation, I decided to go to hypnotherapy. "The Advocate" recommended a lady not too far away. I will refer to her as Mrs. S. It turned out to be the best thing I have ever done. I will walk you through this amazing process and hopefully give you an insight into what is possible. I will caveat this by saying, that if you are going to go to hypnotherapy yourself, I would advise you to skip a few pages here and come back to it once you've been. I don't want to give any readers high expectations. If you walk in expecting to get the experience I had, it may ruin it for you. If you cannot replicate the synergy I had with Mrs. S, you may be found wanting. Also, my mindset was positive going in which could have impacted the results I got.

I made my way to Mrs. S's house, very gingerly and kind of excited. I had no clue what was in store for me; I drove there relatively free of any stress or anxiety. I decided to play a track by one of my favourite artists, Ka. The track is called 'Just'. It holds a very significant meaning for me. At the midpoint, through the track, he delivers what I can only describe as the most heartbreaking and poignant lyrics I think I may have ever heard. I'll divulge those later as well. It was a stunning spring morning in 2021. Although I wasn't in a great place in the lead-up to going to hypnotherapy, I felt pretty good on the day in question. It's almost like I knew in the back of my mind that it would be a positive experience. I didn't get too carried away, as I have had multiple different types of therapy over the years, and nothing had worked. I think being tricked into going to counselling as a teenager affected that. I don't think CBT was ever going to impact me the way it has others, if I am being transparent. Anyway, I am halfway there and listening to my hard-hitting Ka track. As the second verse was coming up, silence ensued. My stereo cut out. Just before he was about to say those bars. I said, "You c*nt." I was completely baffled by how this had happened. Before I had a chance to process it, Google replied to me. "I'm sorry you feel that way." I must have accidentally hit a button on my steering wheel. I erupted in fits of laughter with tears in my eyes while driving down the road. I must have looked completely mental for about five minutes. I couldn't gather myself for quite some time, and I am convinced that moment helped even more. I think it was the way Google replied to me as well; she sounded genuinely hurt by my vulgar language. It was a moment between myself and technology that I'll always find hilarious.

I replayed the track and listened to the song in full just before I pulled up to Mrs. S's house. A wave of nerves came over me, as if I were walking into a world of uncertainty. But then I remembered that today was just the introduction phase, and we wouldn't be going over anything significant. It was more of a meet and greet, plus Mrs. S wanted to know my history, so she had the relevant information to go off and help me move forward. As I was walking up the private drive, I couldn't help but notice how grand all the houses were and how peaceful the setting was. As I approached the door, it felt like time was going in slow motion. I knocked and waited for what was probably a few seconds. Mrs. S opened the door with a glowing smile and said, "Hello, please come in." I stepped through the threshold and felt immediately at ease. Mrs. S had a calm and welcoming demeanor. She guided me through to the room on the right-hand side. I walked in and took a seat.

We spoke for five minutes about the niceties you do when you meet someone new. Like, how are you today? Did you find me okay? She asked why I was there and how she could help. I started to explain and give her a brief outline. She then asked me to give her more potent information about my history. I wasn't closed with any of my responses, as I thought that would do no good. I laid all my cards on the table and gave her my full history from as far back as I could remember. I told her how I felt there was this dark black hole looming over my left shoulder, following me around everywhere I went. Once I had finished rambling on about my less-than-savoury life. Mrs. S was visibly shocked and replied. "Wow! You've been through a lot, haven't you?" I replied "yeah, I suppose I have really. It's not until I talk about it, that I realise I've had far from a normal life". We were supposed to make a recording of this first encounter, however, that never came to fruition. Mrs. S. said, "I think we can start today! How do you feel about that?" I said, "Yeah, I think I can do that. Why not?" Mrs. S smiled and replied, "Great. Ok, well, start by relaxing and getting comfortable. Close your eyes for me. We're going to travel through your timeline. If at any point any of this gets too much, please put your hand up". So, I closed my eyes, and what happened next, I still can't believe.

Mrs. S calmly gets me centered; I then embark on a journey I shall never forget! She said, "Okay, I want you to imagine one line coming out of the front of your forehead, and another line coming out of the back of your head by the crown". Within less than a flicker of a heartbeat, two lines appeared as I visualised them. Mrs. S must have noticed me jolt as it happened, it was so unexpected! She said, "have you got them?" I replied, "Ah, yeah, I have", all confused. "Ok, What colour are they?" she said, I replied with an apprehension in my voice "well, the one at the front is a thin, almost translucent yellow/orange colour, and the one behind is a very thick dark blue". Which, weirdly, was still moving like a dense wave from the ocean. It's hard to explain and do it justice with words alone. I will preface this moment and say, what you're about to read won't be overly easy to digest, and maybe even impossible to accept for some. But I'll do my best. These lines are representative of the past and the future. So, in my case, the past was dark and overbearing, and the future was bleak and held no hope. That's the outlook from my visualisation at that present moment in time. Mrs. S said, "Now I want you to imagine your timeline. Visualise a path that you are going to walk across". I did that; it was like a luminous green walkway that resembled the fret on the Guitar Hero game from years ago. That's the only way I can describe it. Mrs. S then asks me to create a visual bag. She then tells me, as I go along the timeline, put each moment physically in the bag as we proceed, so we can close each bit off as we move on. For some reason, I chose a hessian sack. I'm not sure why? Mrs. S asked me if I was ready to embark on my journey. I replied "yes, I am ready to go". "Ok Ronnie, that's great; we can move on now." That was when she asked me to travel as far back as I could remember. This is where things got strange!

"I want you to go back and visit the youngest version of yourself you can remember. I want you to talk to that little boy for me. Let me know when you get there". Stay with me here. I know this sounds outlandish; I flew there! It felt like I left the room I was sitting in and soared up into the sky. Within seconds, I landed in the Darnley Arms pub car park. But not the version of the pub that still stands there today. I went back to 1989! My brother's shed was still there, as well as the old gravel car park and the weird raised concrete square in the middle, which always reminded me of the Eastenders intro. The black paintwork and all the old benches were outside. It was the most surreal thing I have ever experienced in my entire life.

What occurred next completely blew my mind. I sat on the picnic bench just outside my brother's shed. I watched the five-year-old version of me run out the back door holding a toy. Mrs. S asked me to talk to him. I called him over; it was so real, it was frightening. Actually, frightening isn't the right description. It was more of a celestial experience. The five-year-old version of me ran over and sat on my lap. I ruffled his hair (Yes, I did have some back then). Mrs. S told me to tell him that some things would happen in his life, and that it may be hard going. But he would be okay, he's just got to keep smiling! Make sure he understands. Tears were filling my eyes. It was too much to process in one moment. It was so amazing, yet so upsetting at the same time. Mrs. S asked me if I had done it and said what I needed to say. I replied, that I had, with the same delayed stutter I once had as a five-year-old, which made me slightly confused. Mrs. S then said, "OK, say goodbye to him". I waved at that five-year-old version of me, and he waved back. He ran back inside, through the kitchen door at the back of the pub. He looked back briefly, then disappeared forever.

Mrs. S. asked me to go to the version of me that was the hopeless down-and-out druggy, drinking too much with zero aspirations or direction in life. The version of me that was literally on the brink of suicide! I shot up into the air and went to Meopham. I landed right outside the pathway and looked at the bungalow. Somehow, we had gone from a sunny day in 1989 to this foreboding, early winter evening that harboured a dense mist. The air was so cold, it was like I could reach out and pick ice out of it. I felt strong. I was standing there, angry! Ready to show that skinny little loser inside what was up. I walked up the path with unwavering confidence, twinned with rage. I thumped on the door; the most surreal thing happened. All of a sudden, I could see this scene playing out from a third-person perspective. I saw myself get up and answer the door, at the same time, the 37-year-old man outside was ready to go apeshit on the other side of it. As the door slowly opened, I went straight back to the first person. Standing before my eyes was the weakest, most pathetic excuse of a man I had ever seen in my entire life. He looked frail, rejected and afraid. I put my hand out to stop him from closing the door on me; I immediately picked up on his fear. I trod over the doorstep, grabbed the 31-year-old version of me by the neck, and slammed him up against the wall on the landing. I had picked him up off the floor with both hands as I hoisted him up in the air by the collar. I was shouting at him, telling him to sort his fucking life out. The version that was looking back at me was crying and shaking, non-responsive to my rage, shelled up in terror. While all this was going on, I could feel my eyes welling up again with tears.

Mrs. S decided to intervene and change the trajectory of what was happening. I didn't know if I was acting this all out in her room. Which was weird, but it felt so real. She said, "Ok, what's going on?" I said what I had done to him. She calmly replied, "before you leave, you have to do it on good terms. I know you might not want to. But it's important for the rest of the timeline". I then turned the violent hold I had on him into a hug and said, "you have got to sort it out mate. You're going to end up like your brother. Is that what you fucking want? To do that to your sister again? Come on, think about this. Go and get yourself together. You're better than all this". The 31-year-old me looked back, hugged me, agreed, and tremblingly walked back into his room.

Now, this bit freaks me out more than anything else. I don't know if any of you reading this book have seen the film Deja Vu with Denzel Washington. If you haven't, then please watch it after you've finished reading my book. It's a remarkable piece of cinematography. If you recall, I mentioned earlier in the book that I sat down in my bedroom and wrote a note with my aspirations for 2016. This was where I felt like I went back in time and stopped myself from picking up the right-hand side of that note (Kill yourself). I went back to a third person; it was as if there was something or someone else watching over me. I felt another presence, as if I were looking through a lens from the past, that somehow was in real-time. I must have been so far under, I transitioned for a brief spell. I then watched both versions of myself walk off in different directions, respectively. The little, weak "man" shut the door, sat down, and carried on writing his list. The angry, real man walked back down that frosty, dark pathway, like that guy in a movie walking away from a colossal explosion! I came away from the house and despite both leaving that particular scene, let's call it a scene, as that is what it felt like. I just stood there and observed them both via this unerringly, disturbing optical viewpoint. I was watching myself cry my eyes out onto a piece of paper but seeing him realise that the left-hand side of that sheet was the only choice, and simultaneously watching myself standing outside my old bungalow, feeling exhilarated!

Mrs. S said, "Okay, well done. I now need you to come back to the present". So, I put that horrific part of the story in my hessian sack and moved forward. At this point, it felt as if I was astral projecting, or part of the most incredible computer game ever made. Mrs. S asked me how I felt, I said I was okay. But I was a bit taken back. We worked on some current stuff. She asked about my goals and what I was focusing on at that moment. I explained to her that music and fitness was a huge part of my life. "That's amazing," she said. "It's great you have hobbies. I'd like you to put your energy in a positive place. So, let's work on a tiny hint of the future". She said to visualise what you want from your music. Think of where you're heading in the next couple of months. I was still in this deep, trance-like state of mind. So, I did just that. Mrs. S gave me a few minutes to bask in that moment and said, "OK, Ronnie. How's the black hole over your left shoulder looking now?" I said it had shrunk, a little bewildered... Then she asked how the lines were now coming

144

from the front and back of my head after the session. I said, "Oh wow! The yellow one in front is massive and bright; it almost resembles the shape of a Wi-Fi signal. The blue line at the back is ultra-thin and has this smokey consistency". Mrs. S said, "Open your eyes". I opened them, full of confusion. I suddenly leapt into a barrage of questions for her. I said, "what just happened? I don't understand it". She smiled and lifted her arm, and said, "I have got goosebumps. That was extraordinary! I rarely get someone with the visual powers you have." We were both smiling. I couldn't make head or tail of anything. I kept quizzing her. She was almost laughing at this point, as I couldn't grasp the reality of what had gone on. We spoke for about fifteen minutes. Mrs. S explained how well I had done, and how much I managed to immerse myself in each moment. I couldn't verbalise how I felt.

I approached hypnotherapy with an open mind, but I never expected it to have such a life-altering effect. It doesn't mean it'll do that for everybody. But, from personal experience, I can't think of anything that comes close. I turned up at Mrs. S's place at 10:00 a.m. I was told beforehand that it would take around 45 minutes to an hour long each session. When I stepped out of her door, I looked up and was in complete awe of my surroundings. Everything was in high definition and resembled being in a 3D Cinema. I mean, I could see the details on the leaves. I was like a blind man that had just been granted vision. I looked across the road at my car. It was like it was right in front of me. As I walked across her driveway, I looked around at different objects, to see what intricacies I could gather through my optics. I checked my phone to see if I had any messages or missed calls and checked the time. It was 11:45 a.m. I could not believe my eyes. I got in my car to double-check. It was right. I had been under for over an hour and a half. It honestly felt like half an hour. I came out of there a different person, I honestly did. That moment truly was the turning point for me, to get my mental health back on track. It was the perfect steppingstone to finally move on with life. The past is the past. Unfortunately, as much as most of us would like to go back and at least change one thing, we can't! I'd change a good few, but then, I suppose, as long as you learn from it and stay mindful moving forward, that is the best thing to do. After that session, I found another level of confidence and got to grips with being happy alone. It isn't easy for someone like me who has spent large periods of their life in relationships or surrounded by friends every weekend. If you can understand how to be happy alone, like I have recently, then it's a superpower!

Three weeks later and I am back in hypnotherapy. I am filled with nothing but excitement this time around. I know what to expect to a certain degree and couldn't wait to get started. Mrs. S asked how I had been after the first session. I needed those weeks for my brain to recover, and settle down again, so I could process the ordeal I had been through. I only needed one more, as we covered a vast amount the first time. Because I was so deep into the process, she didn't want to break the connection. In a way, that was ultimately the best thing for me. Although it did hit me afterwards; as I thought I was slightly mental! Even talking about it now, I am hyper-alert as to how bat-shit crazy it must sound. But I can only tell you what happened to me in there. Now, going back was a weird one, to be honest. I had expectations this time. I desperately tried not to have them. But it was impossible. Even though it was more recent; I can't remember that session in as much detail as the first. I'm honestly baffled as to why that is. Maybe it's because the first session was a brand-new experience!

This time, she wanted me to do some tapping, which is literally what it says on the tin. You tap all your sensory points and repeat some mantras to get the brain focused and heighten your senses. We went through that for around five minutes. Then I went back to my timeline and planted the seed. The idea was to reverse the negative connotations attached to so many moments of my past. So, I planted the "metaphorical seed" for this new plant 'new me' to grow. I walked through my timeline once more with a positive outlook on matters, and shed some light through the murky clouds that have followed me around. The lines were how I left them from my last session, just slightly more pronounced. The one in front was huge and fluorescent yellow. The one behind me was a thin shadowy blue colour. I was walking up this bright green, luminescent pathway. Instead of my hessian bag, I was observing the plant slowly grow as I moved up towards the present day. I was incrementally talking my past out of existence, and my future into reality. Mrs. S was very confident and said to turn that small plant into a tree, to make the positive thoughts more powerful! So, I did just that. Then out of nowhere, with absolutely zero warning, the tree went black and started to creep over me. It turned into a horror film. I said, "Ah. Nope. No, this isn't good". It was like being in a sunken place. Mrs. S raised her voice gently and advised me to go back to the plant. Luckily, I got out of whatever darkness I fell into at that moment. We resumed the session. This time, it was very different. We were just putting the finishing touches on what we built in the first time around. I was steaming through and heading towards the present rapidly!

Mrs.' S then threw a curve ball at me and said, "Now I want you to imagine yourself performing your music and picture yourself on stage. Choose someone who has inspired you recently and whom you can almost emulate. Maybe you could even be performing with them in this vision". I picked Black Thought from the Roots. One of his live performances wowed me at the time. So, I pictured myself on stage with The Roots. We were rapping together, it was incredible! I looked out into the crowd and saw seas of people cheering. Then I noticed the floor I was standing on was the same floor that is featured in my timeline. It was a luminous green, there were pulsing lights rushing through it. I felt like electricity was coursing through my veins. It was such a surreal experience. I was brimming with confidence. Going toe to toe, performing with one of the greatest to ever rap, I fully embraced the moment, like it was genuinely happening right there and then. The crowd were on their feet, cheering. I could feel the atmosphere. Mrs. S. then calmly said, "Open your eyes". That is what I find the hardest to fathom, whilst I am so deeply engrossed in what's going on in my visualisations, yet I am still responsive to Mrs. S's voice. But I suppose that's the idea, isn't it? I looked at Mrs. S; she had goosebumps again. It was an otherworldly experience. She said "we're done! "I said, forever?" She laughed and said, "for the immediate future Ronnie".

When I left, I almost floated out of the door. It's like I cut off that gloomy hole looming and forever present over my shoulder. I had a sense of freedom and peace. I didn't realise such a feeling was attainable via hypnotherapy. I wish I'd known much sooner. But timing is everything; it was the right time for me to embark on such a mission. I owe all of this to "The Advocate". After coming out of hypnotherapy, I decided it was imperative to start being more mindful of my thoughts and feelings and try to actively combat them daily. Rather than let myself sink into a place of disorder and uncertainty. Mrs. S gave me a sheet to take away, with a list of things to read daily if I wanted. I did, very diligently.

I will leave some of the things listed below as I feel they are important. We forget about the basics these days, as life is flying at a relentless pace. We rarely get a chance to ask ourselves if we're okay. 'Breathe deeply'. This is one that I still do a few times a week. It's quite enlightening just how breathing deeply for a minute or so can change your mood and put you into a state of calmness. 'Eating healthily' is one that many of us neglect, as we rarely have time to cook fresh. We're all either too tired or too busy. A poor diet can drag the body down very quickly! If your body isn't functioning right, your mind won't be that far behind, trust me! 'Getting good sleep' This is probably the most important thing for someone who's bordering on insomnia. I find this one the toughest to achieve. 'Think about three people who inspire you daily'; it can be the same three people, or three different people every day. If there's an author you admire or a friend who is doing something like running a marathon or starting a business. Maybe a musician who inspires you? It could be anything or anyone! Exercise. Now, I exercise most days. I've learned a lot about physical and mental health over the last four or five years. The body should run parallel with the mind to be in perfect harmony and be happy. You don't have to bust a gut for two hours daily in the gym. Maybe go for a brisk walk, or do yoga for an hour. I have kept on top of all these things, much better than I could have ever done before. Mrs. S had given me strategies and the knowledge to achieve such things. So, I felt it was up to me to run with that and try and put those things to good use. I was still adapting to being alone after splitting up with

Anna. I had finally found myself; So, I decided a new challenge was in order.

Chapter 14

A Bump In The Road

So, the challenge… It's one I had been mulling over for a few years. One I was honestly scared of but determined to achieve. I have realised that since relinquishing the buzz I got from drugs and pushing my body to its absolute limit. I can't help but crave some sort of danger and put myself in a degree of jeopardy. It keeps me feeling alive. It would also explain my interest in the more extreme urban sports that I partook in as a youngster. I know that probably doesn't resonate with many of you, and you can quite happily go about life without experiencing such madness. But I'm not built like that. I wish I was sometimes. It'd be a lot easier for me. Now that I had acquired my black belt in Japanese kickboxing in the early part of 2016. Unfortunately, the injuries that came with it, prevented me from carrying on. Years went by until I discovered Krav, then when that shut down, due to the "Pandemic" I felt a bit empty and had to address what I had not previously in Kickboxing. I had never fought Ross, as I got injured before getting the chance to. I felt like a fraud. No one else ever seemed to think so. Well, they didn't say so anyway.

So, in January 2021. I decided to approach Ross one day. We were just standing in his kitchen having a coffee, and I blurted it out. "I want to do my 2nd Dan Black Belt". Ross was taken back slightly and replied. "Ok, do you have a date in mind?" We agreed that mid-May was a good time to aim for. There was a catch, it was bare-knuckle. I knew this, but I was willing to put my body at risk once more, because I never learn! I began training. It was an anxiety-filled few months. I couldn't relax at all, as I knew what was coming. Closer to the date, I started to tell a few friends in my immediate circle, to make it real. I was excited as well as scared. Also, it held me accountable and gave me an extra layer of proof, that I was going to fulfill my potential and stick to my word.

I had thirty-six new techniques to learn, and I had to prepare myself for bare-knuckle, write a new kata and break some thick slate roof tiles. I started to go on long walks to help clear my mind and mentally zone in for what was coming. Also, by proxy, it was keeping me quite fit. I turned the tunes on, walked across all my local fields, and through a golf course a few times a week. I'd find myself taking a seat in a graveyard of all places, half-way through my walks. I never contemplated why that was until right this second. Maybe it was a subconscious decision, where I was surrounded by death and that we only get one go round, so to make the most of it? Plus, the dead are quieter! I knuckled down and spent a lot of time alone. Getting myself fit and practicing for what was to come. I was still partaking in Calisthenics to keep fit and strong. I zoned in for my 2nd Dan Black Belt and I was hell bent on success.

Although, there would be a massive distraction, as the universe had other plans in store for me. Nothing ever goes the way we expect it too sometimes. I have learned this the hard way, more often than not over the years. It's made me more vigilant and adaptable to circumstances that arise. You can't expect a perfect linear trajectory towards your destination. There'll always be adversity, hurdles, and a spanner thrown in the works at some stage. It's how you navigate around it that matters. Let's call this particular instance, a life lesson. That came in the form of a lady called Alice. She appeared in my life one day. I was over at Ross' house; we were doing some kickboxing pad-work in his front room. Alice, knocked on the door. Bearing this in mind, I had known Ross for well over a decade. Unbelievably, I had never met his sister-in-law. As soon as she turned up, I was like, oh, she's pretty. As we were training, she was in the loft gathering some of the stuff she had left there from a previous house move. After an hour or so, Alice comes down and joins us for a cup of tea. Ross gets an important phone call from work, and we're left sitting on the sofa.

Naturally, being a gobby git, I strike up a conversation, make polite chit-chat, and ask what she does for work. She divulges that she is a police officer; to which I jokingly went to walk out the door. We hit it off well. Ross comes back and says, "You better not be chatting up my sister-in-law." I reply, "As if I would," and laugh. Alice starts packing up her car, and it quickly becomes apparent that she needed to make multiple trips. Ross bundles through the door and asks if I can assist. I go outside to help her pack, Alice then grabs a skateboard out of the car, I laugh and say, "I didn't have you down as a skater". She replied, "I haven't got a clue how to do it. My daughter wants to learn, so I bought one to go with her". I thought that was very sweet and told her so. I wanted to jump on the skateboard and relive my youth. We were on a ramp, and I thought, if I crack my head open, that's a surefire way to look like a complete fool! So, I resisted and put it back in the boot. Alice asked if I was any good. I humbly replied that I used to be, back in my teenage years. I was fighting every instinct in my body not to grab the skateboard back out of the car.

Without further ado, we all left to drop the stuff off at Alice's temporary place. When we arrived, Ross and I grabbed some stuff and helped carry it into the garage. I saw the skateboard again. But this time, I was on level ground. Temptation, and my inner child just got the better of me. I put it on the floor and said, "do you mind?" Alice said "no, course not, go ahead!" I only pulled off a kickflip! I was shocked! Ross was like, "How the hell can you still do that?" I smirked and said, "It never left me." Alice looked quite impressed, and said, "I know who I'm asking for lessons". Whilst Ross stood in the background, shaking his head in disapproval. I grinned and winked at him.

When we got back in the car, he was like, "You fucker!" I chuckled away, quietly proud of myself. We said our goodbyes and went our separate ways. Ross then told me how she hadn't long split up from her husband, hence all the moving boxes around. My ears pricked up with curiosity. But for once, I managed to keep my mouth shut. We headed back to Ross' house, chilled for a bit, and watched a film. Rozzy came home, and Ross immediately said, "By the way, you have got a new brother-in-law and laughed". She didn't look overly pleased, and I said, "don't worry, I won't break her heart". She said, "It would more likely be the other way around. Plus, she has a kid. If you are willing to take on that responsibility again?" I didn't say anything more, other than make a few light-hearted jokes. If only I had listened! I suppose I was judging her off what Rozzy is like. She is a wholesome, lovely, and trustworthy woman.

A few days later I was at work, when I got a message from Ross saying Alice had asked for my number. I immediately said "Yes, give it to her". Now, I should have run the moment she first called me. It was a video call; she was very intoxicated. Alarm bells did go off big time; I justified it and maybe thought she just was nervous. In reality that should have been enough to say, don't go there. Anyway, I don't want to put too much credence into this situation, as it was largely negative. Alice and I saw each other for about five months. During that period, she had never stopped seeing her husband, and apparently, another guy was on the scene. I was angry, because I told her I had mental health issues and had not long come out of a volatile relationship with Anna. It didn't seem to matter to her, she did a huge number on me and led me to believe she loved me. Oh well, we live and learn.

I eventually walked away and gave myself the respect I deserved! I haven't spoken to her since, despite her indirect efforts to lure me back. I harbour no ill feelings towards her. I've not exactly been a patron saint. It wasn't a wasted five months; it taught me a lot about myself. It made me realise that it's not ever happening again with her or any other woman who acts that way. She's not a bad person; she's just a bit lost. Haven't we all felt lost at some point? I could seldom allow myself to get down about it. I had bigger things to worry about, that came in the shape of an 83Kg man, with fists like shovels.

The grading for my 2nd Dan was only weeks away now, I had all this, plus Alice rushing through my head. But I did have the habit of making things harder for myself; a sick part of me welcomed the extra challenge. Again, I go back to my old adage of, If I could achieve this under such stress, nothing can stop me! It's a weird mentality, but it's just like when I gave up smoking not long after my dad passed. If you can do something in the toughest situations, it makes you unbreakable! Typical me, though. Just when I got my life together, all this drama unfolded. For once though, the vast majority of it wasn't my fault.

I was due to grade on Saturday, May 13th, 2021. Then, out of the blue, I got a phone call from Ross on the Thursday beforehand. I knew what was coming. He said his old favourite saying. "You want to eat the frog and get this done tonight?". It was not what I had planned, but my exact words were. "Fuck it, let's do it." It was two days less anxiety, and it was better to get it over and done with. I didn't tell a single soul. Not even my sister. It put the power back in my hands, and I was now in full control of my destiny! I could go and do the grading without any extra pressure on my shoulders. Which was nice because I hadn't felt that for two months prior.

There were around eight hours to get my head together and go through all the stuff I had been learning over the last four months or so. The pressure was on. Luckily, the weather was on our side, so we decided to do the grading outside under some trees. The setting was pretty cool; it had a Mortal Kombat feel to it. I got there first and warmed up, pacing up and down like a polar bear in a zoo. The light was starting to fade as it was coming up to 8:30 p.m. fortunately, it was approaching summer, and the nights were a little more forgiving. I saw Ross come around the corner. "Right, this is it. Switch on and look lively!" I anxiously muttered to myself. We started with the techniques. There were a few I was still struggling with the mechanics of, but for some reason, I managed to nail them on the night. I think it was sheer determination, focus and not wanting to mess it up.

Once I had completed that phase, it was onto the Kata. I annoyingly stuttered on one move, but it was decent other than that. Then it was time to chuck the gum shield in and put a bit of Vaseline on our faces. Honestly, it was just our faces! I was shitting myself! Ross admitted it later on, he was a little nervous too due to being out of action for so long himself. For those of you who don't know what Kumite is, it's one 7-minute round with no breaks. No protective gear is worn, other than a gum-shield. It's bare-knuckle, and the fight isn't over until either someone is knocked out, or the timer comes to an end. There are limited rules; pretty much anything goes. Headbutts, elbows, knees, kicks to the groin and your standard punches to anywhere and everywhere! We had a gentleman's agreement that there was no need for the shots to the northern regions, especially unprotected. It seemed a little unnecessary. Although it would have been much less stressful if I had kicked him in the balls.

The Kumite starts, Ross is a much taller and a bigger guy in general. My game plan was wrong! I decided to go with a lower center of gravity, keep everything tight, and fight off the counter in the hope I either wouldn't get chinned or dropped in the first minute. I came to survive it and land what I could. I adopted a more Krav Maga approach with my footwork and high guard. Looking back, I wish I'd gone out on my shield more and gotten stuck in! But after the bad injuries before, I thought that was probably foolish in the current circumstances. I had a job role where a functional body comes into play much more often than not. Two minutes in, and I get dropped with a huge leg kick. I get up after a few seconds and carry on. One minute later, a shot straight into the nuts (accidental) Ross pauses the timer, I get up again. I catch a few heavier shots, but nothing to wipe me out. I think I may have gotten him with a good body shot and one that clipped him up top, and that was it.

Reflecting on it now, it would have been better if I fought someone I didn't know or someone that I hated. That way, I could have just gone full-out with no emotion. The timer goes off, we embrace, probably both feeling a bit of relief. I was not aware of this beforehand, but the main purpose is to show you have the minerals to get in there in the first place and do it. I theoretically could have tapped out in the first 10 seconds and still passed. Not knowing that information before made zero difference to me anyway. I couldn't have lived with myself if I bowed out like a coward. The whole point was to show I was brave enough to step up and take my inevitable kick in like a man. It wasn't over, I still had to do my tile break. When I purchased these tiles, I was conscious that they were extremely thick. They weren't the ones I had broken for my 1st Dan grading. But Ross, with his forever-optimistic outlook, assured me it would be fine. I wasn't so sure. They were rock-solid and all around 3 mm each. When we got back to mine, Ross set up the break outside my back door. He rightly suggested a warm-up, and put two tiles over the bricks, ready for me to hit. I only had a hand wrap on, so there wasn't much protection. I stepped up to the first two tiles and broke them with relative ease. I will say now that there were no spacers between the tiles like there were on my 1st Dan grading, as Ross was adamant that was the rule for 2nd Dan. Which later came to light may have well been wrong. Cheers mate!

Ross asked me how I was, and I said, "yeah, I'm ok, but they're solid". I was supposed to do ten but being a lower weight than a select few before who had done it, it would have caused a massive discrepancy if I were to do the same. So, I think it was five or six tiles in the end. I stepped up once more and centered myself to strike. I gave them a proper clump and heard them explode! I immediately felt a huge amount of pain in my right hand. Ross jumped up and was more excited than he normally was. Which is no mean feat by any stretch of the imagination. He bellowed out. "You dim-maked them." Dim-mak means a touch of death. It's where you strike through the target so fast, breaking the tiles at the bottom of the pile and not at the top. I let out a brief cheer, then I was then quickly drawn back to the excruciating pain in my right hand. I noticed a massive bulge sticking out the back of it, protruding through the hand wrap. I held it up, and Ross said, "Okay, don't panic. But it looks like you've broken your hand there, mate". We went upstairs to my kitchen; Ross asked me to lay my hand flat on the kitchen worktop. He then pushed it back in with all his weight, as if you were about to do CPR. I grimaced, whilst listening to all the parts crunching around like a box of kid's toys. Ross delivered the good news - I still had to go back outside to complete my tile break. I thought he was joking at first, but he was deadly serious.

156

I went back downstairs and did what I set out to do. I was not going to let this stop me from passing. Even if I had to headbutt them. Ross said, "rather than potentially breaking your other hand, why don't you axe-kick them instead to complete it?" So, without barely taking a breath, I walked up to them and smashed through them with an axe kick. At this point, I was past caring and wanted to achieve my goal. Well, I got my 2nd Dan Black Belt. But I was back out of action for a few weeks with my 'professor Klump-hand'. When we arrived back at Ross' house to celebrate and have a takeaway, I spent about an hour writing a message to people telling them I passed my grading. That wasn't easy with one hand, but I knew it wouldn't be much better in the coming days. I couldn't wait to share my joy and pain!

Everyone was very supportive, I got loads of great messages from my closest friends. The next morning, my hand was like a balloon. I had to go to the hospital. I couldn't drive, so I got a lift and went for an X-ray. I was fully expecting to have the news that I had broken my hand and that I would be rendered a bit useless for a while. The doctor came out and said, "You are so lucky! I can't believe you haven't broken it". I said, "Are you sure? How is that possible?" She said I had just smashed all the cartilage out the back of my hand and that it all gone back into place. Well, pushed! "It's very swollen, so don't hit anything for at least three months". I took her advice but was back doing Calisthenics within a couple of weeks. It was funny because Sel works in the Hospital, and they got someone to deliver a message to me on how to punch properly, which was nice. I was already on holiday from work as I had the foresight to know that something could well go wrong. The time off came as a blessing in disguise, because I was going hell for leather in training and had a few niggly injuries in various places of my body. So, being forced to sit my arse down for a while was a welcome break!

A couple of weeks later, I am getting back in the game. I'm on top of my job, I'm back doing what I love. Writing new tracks for my albums and knocking goals off my list almost weekly. I was also getting into wild camping. It was nice to have a new hobby that wasn't detrimental to my health in some way. Ross,

Ricksta and I head out one night. It was the first time those guys had met, they got on like a house on fire. We stopped at a garage to grab some bits; out of nowhere… "The Advocate" appears before me, looking incredible! She was all dressed up; I had no words. I fumbled and jittered and fell over every syllable like a child. To top it all off, I looked like a bag of shit. My beard was all over the place. I had crappy clothes on due to camping. We were both in a state of shock, as we hadn't seen each other for a while at this particular time. Due to both going through messy break ups with our ex-partners. She went as bright red as me. We fired a few messages back and forth after our brief encounter. I did have to tell her via message once I got to camp, how stunning she looked. "The Advocate" was her usual lovely self, and that was that. We rekindled after that fleeting moment. It was a really bizarre point in my life, of strangely timed events, and that remained the theme of 2021.

The rest of the year was still at my disposal. I was trying to regain some level of focus. I was lacking a bit of direction, and for some reason, I was amidst an existential crisis. You know those moments where you're sitting there and just think, What the fuck am I doing here? What is life all about? Am I even on the right track, or am I a fraud, an imposter? A man who is living someone else's life. Well, that's what I was dealing with at the time.

Now I double back, I can see that it was probably a combination of things. With it being so quiet and unable to see anyone, as we were still living in the aftermath of the "Pandemic", I suppose it was natural to turn the mirror on yourself more often than not. It was a huge segment our lives, where we were with our thoughts and feelings much more than we would have been in busy years past. It's not a great thing for me, to be brutally honest. I regularly struggled bouncing around in my head; it can be dangerous up there at the best of times. I thought I better channel these thoughts into something positive and concentrate on what I wanted for the rest of 2021. I had some unfinished, yet grand and sporadic ideas for tattoos. I thought it was a good time to go on a tattoo-designing mission, as work was dead. I had loads of free time on my hands. It was a welcome invitation to take my mind off the inner fears and anxieties I was currently experiencing.

So, I got to work. I had quite a few ideas for a new back piece. I had a big Millwall Lion on my back to cover, this made the whole process much more complicated than just a normal back tattoo. I spoke to a few people; everyone said there was a good possibility that it could be covered. But with what? I knew it was going to be music-related, as I wanted some lyrics written on me. Those lyrics are still, to this day, my favourite of all time; "Trying to find a reason, I'm still alive breathing. I wanna heal my inner child. It's been a while grieving". Absolute magic! Honestly, I have never heard my life summed up in a couple of sentences so perfectly. If you are wondering? Yes! they were the lyrics from the song I was listening to on the way to my first Hypnotherapy session. They are now permanently part of me. Those lyrics were off an album called Honor Killed The Samurai. That's when it hit me. I was at work; I thought to myself... Samurai. They're lone warriors who fight to the death. Which I can relate to. I have always been a fan of martial arts films and imagery. Plus, The Wu-Tang Clan regularly uses samples of that nature in their music. My next thought was ah... I could have a Samurai on my back with those lyrics. Then, I concluded that as I grew up in the countryside and do wild camping. That it would be very fitting to have a Samurai standing in the woods with those lyrics written amongst the trees. I was so excited, I frantically searched Google for images. I've never been one for just copying and pasting an image where tattoos are concerned. So many people out there have that covered for me. I typed in Samurai standing in the woods to give me some rough ideas on what I could get. I found the perfect image within five minutes, that I could use as a reference point. I instantly knew it was the way to go. I spent the whole afternoon piecing together bits, and then once I got to a place where I was happy with it, I texted my tattooist to find out when they were reopening. It was only a matter of months. I was over the moon. Other than the little issue of it costing an absolute fortune! It was all coming together amazingly. Whilst on Google I kept wading through different images and websites.

This is when I stumbled upon a gentleman called Miyamoto Musashi. I had no clue how much this great man would impact

159

my life. As I delved further into what was a never-ending rabbit hole, I discovered that Miyamoto Musashi was more than just a Samurai - he was an author, philosopher, and strategist. There was something very profound that I read - the 21 rules of life. I resonated with 20 of them. I started researching him more deeply and found an endless pool of unlimited greatness. I watched a few YouTube videos about his life. An hour later, and after much research. I knew I was on the right path and that it was not by chance. It was fate that I found him.

The extensional crisis I was going through was short-lived. I had the answers, not only for my tattoo, but for my path. I was on the right track. Miyamoto Musashi captured my imagination, as I always felt like a bit of a lone warrior to a degree and fought for everything I ever had. I found it enthralling and incredibly inspirational, how he took himself off to be completely alone, to fight to the death in 60 duels and kill every one of his adversaries to remain undefeated. His story of self-mastery and the way he approached life were nothing short of admirable. It was one of those life-changing epiphany moments. It's hard to describe but knew I would be fine treading the uneasy road that lay before me. Whilst being able accomplish what I needed to do without any reliance on anyone else or anything external. It came at the perfect time as well. It was just after my 2nd Dan grading it all snapped into place. For the first time, Hip Hop, martial arts, my tattoos, and my journey were all linked. I had no doubts that I was exactly where I was supposed to be.

I was naturally excited to share this story with Ross. He had witnessed this part of my life and was privy to my situation. On my first day off I went over to his to train some Calisthenics. I was like a cat on a hot tin roof. "Mate, I have something to tell you". I was so overly exuberant I could barely construct an English sentence. I said "I have had an epiphany moment. You won't believe this". I told him what I had discovered at work and how I knew I was on the right path. I explained how I had read this intriguing article and watched videos about a Japanese Samurai, and how It all linked my entire existence together. All of a sudden. He said, "STOP THERE!" He disappeared into his front room. I heard him searching for something. He came back in with a smile and handed me a book. "Is that him?" The book he handed me was 'The Book of Five Rings by Miyamoto Musashi'. What Ross said next nearly made me pass out. "You have to read that before your 3rd Dan grading. I wasn't going to give that to you for at least another year. But seeing as you discovered it yourself. Here you go!" I couldn't speak, move, or do anything for at least ten seconds. All he got back was a "Yeah" … My eyes were bulging out of my head in utter disbelief that this was even happening. It just further reinforced everything tenfold. I didn't know whether to laugh or cry. Then I erupted like a volcano of vocabulary and bounced around his kitchen like Zebedee. After I had managed to pull myself down from the ceiling, Ross turned around and said, "I'm not sure how I feel about that, to be honest." We were both in a state of shock! I'll never forget that day as long as I live. It was all I needed to be even more sure about my unpredictable journey. I had no doubts about ringing the tattooist.

My first session was penciled in for September, and I couldn't wait. I had three full-day sessions booked within three months. I was determined to get it done as quickly as possible. The bipolar roller coaster that was my life seemed to be on the up again. Everything had come full-circle. Things came together in the most unforeseen way. Despite being relieved that I had all the answers that plagued me for so long. I unexpectedly found happiness in solitude, which had eluded me for over two decades. I never can still can fully relax due to the nature of my life. It's so frustrating to have had pessimism as a default setting for so long. But I suppose I can forgive myself for that because of what I have been through. These days, I don't let it determine my mindset. Even as recently as 2021. I hadn't managed to conquer those persistent ups and downs. It had been a relatively good year. There were bumps in the road relationship-wise, but nothing too debilitating. Or so I thought...

Then, dreaded October comes, which seems to be an unlucky month for me for some reason. I came home from work one night; I got off the train and went to get my car to drive home. I was walking up the road very tired and pressing my key fob to no avail! When I parked at 5:20 am. I was always half asleep, and I had misplaced it once or twice before. So, I started to walk back down the road parallel. As soon as I came around the corner, I saw my car in front of me, parked on double yellow lines facing the other way. I was so confused. I thought I didn't park there. I walked around the front of the car to find there was no front end left on it. Someone had moved it and stripped it. I put my bag on the floor and stared at it in shock. I didn't even know what to do. After a few minutes trying to grasp what had happened, I rang the police. Then I rang my insurance company, who were shut, obviously, at 8:30 pm. Then I thought I better try and get home. I rang my sister; she was out with friends. My mate Cindy kindly gave me a lift home. I rang my boss to tell him I obviously wouldn't be in the next day as I had to sort this mess out. He said, "no problem, I'll ring the area manager and tell him you won't be in". I got a message back in about 15 minutes saying I'd receive disciplinary if I failed to go in the next day. My boss was livid he got that response. As was I. There's nothing like a bit of moral support, is there? I was close to saying, tell him to get fucked. But, out of spite and to show him up to everyone I decided to put my ego to one side and attend work the next day. I was smart and calm and played the game for once. It didn't matter much. I had to get Ubers' for about a month anyway. From that day on nobody liked him or respected him at all. He "left" anyway! I remember all through that week commencing, looking up thinking, really! What else?

A few days go by, and I get an email from "The Advocate" I was happy to hear from her, but the circumstances were less than favourable. One of the guys from "Fight Club" had been killed in a motorbike accident. I texted her on WhatsApp. We chatted for a bit and had a good catch-up. although I didn't know the guy particularly well, it was unfortunate news to hear. "The Advocate" and I were in contact quite a bit again, I was happy to have her back in my life properly. Then she weaves another bit of magic. I was in a slight lull, and She suggested that I should talk to her mum, who is a higher medium. I was even more sceptical of Mediums than Hypnotherapists, to be honest. Although, I was willing to try and keep the same open mind I did when I saw Mrs. S. All I had to do was select a date before the end of the year. I chose December 5th, my mum's birthday. I didn't tell a soul. Not even "The Advocate". I was extremely nervous.

We had not long come out of Covid, so the reading was to be over a video call. You would assume, that surely, it would be more difficult to grab detail; with me not being in her presence. I'm not sure? Also, I don't exist on any social media platform to gather information. "The Advocate" had never told her my story. Thirty seconds into the call, Sandra jolts and says someone is here already! That is unusual. She identifies a female presence and then stops briefly. "Ah, your mums here". Then asks me if there is a reason for her immediate contact. I apprehensively replied, "It's my Mum's birthday today". She smiled and said "ah... Ok, that makes sense now". I still wasn't fully invested at this stage. Then Sandra turned around less than ten seconds later and said, "your dad is here now". I started feeling a little odd. What was to come next left no doubt in my mind. I was witnessing something from a completely different world. Sandra looks at me and says "you've got siblings. They're older; there is a disconnection. A blurred line, something's wrong. Do you not talk to one of them? Oh wait... Your brother is here". Sandra knew something was wrong and how he died. She raised one of her hands to her throat and said "I'm getting a strong pain in my neck. Did he..." I said "yes, he took his own life when I was twelve". I am now in uncontrollable tears and can't believe what is occurring in front of my eyes. Sandra relays a message. "Your brother wants to know where his watch is. He isn't mad if you have sold it". I said "no, no, it's in the kitchen cupboard. The battery leaked in the back of it, I was unable to get it repaired". There's no way she could have known this information. It was the only thing he left me when he died. She then smiled and said, "he's asked for a fag, cheeky sod, isn't he?" I laughed through the tears and said, "that sounds like him". As a reader of this book, you're probably still sceptical. If you haven't been convinced by now, then you will be by the time you have read the next paragraph.

Sandra then goes on to give me a message from my dad. My dad was a Cockney and had a specific way with words. Sandra is a Scouser, and I have never heard her phrase anything like the way she did, when she relayed this message. He was the only man I know who could have said that sentence the way Sandra told me. "Son, I'm really proud of you, keep doing your music. Make sure you get it out there". As you know, my mother passed away, and we weren't talking at the time. Sandra said, "Your mum is desperate for me to tell you something". "She said she is sorry. It wasn't your fault what happened to David. She was just angry. She also says you are a very special boy, and that you were her miracle baby". I had a complete breakdown at this point. That was the moment, if there was any doubt, it was removed with that sentence. I remember when I was around twelve or thirteen, sitting next to my mum and her saying those exact words to me. Only my dad and sister could have known this; I have never told anyone she said that. The final few messages were from my brother saying to stay away from Anna. He said she's no good for you, and I am to move on! I think he probably noticed it was a similar pattern to his disastrous relationship with his ex. He'd have been correct!

What happened next was truly heartfelt and left me feeling a degree of peace I hadn't experienced since that near-fatal day back in 2017, when I briefly tripped over the line between life and death. It was a message from all my family, reiterating not to blame myself for what had gone on in the past. That I was just a kid. I had been carrying guilt, grief, misery, and pain around like a lead-weight for two decades and couldn't get it to leave me be. For the first time, I was free in life, not duty-bound by the trauma, that ate away at my soul. I owe that to "The Advocate" and Sandra. I was a caged animal for years, that had just been released back into the wild. I rang Tracey afterwards to tell her about the reading and how blown away I was. I asked her if she remembered that mum called me her miracle baby. She didn't even know herself! What a way to end a crazy year of ups and downs.

When 2022 dawned, I thought, you know what, I will try and put my affinity to one side for "The Advocate". She deserves to find peace within herself after so much heartache. I wanted to make sure she was ok more than anything in the world. I turned my attention to my new list of yearly goals. "The Advocate" was bouncing back strong, and she seemed happy. We were becoming closer and closer by the week, talking all the time. We were both re-finding our feet after bad relationship experiences. We had two shockers one after another and were both treading similarly uneven, but better grounds. Even though we had each other to call in a time of need, I have also become incredibly aware lately that no matter how close you are with anyone in the world, it is important to remember that some people come into your life for a reason, a season, or a lifetime only time will tell which one. However hard it may be to deal with.

I start the year off well. Every New Year the first thing on my list, without question, is to look after my mental health. That is paramount, and I realise that now. Because without good mental health, you are doing nothing! So, I make that my number one priority. I think now is a good time to point out that I haven't got here all alone. It would be remise of me to pretend otherwise. I have acknowledged a lot of friends and loved ones so far. I think now is the perfect time to acknowledge someone who has become an older brother figure in my life. Deano. He has helped me through so much in the last couple of years. We've had some real heart-to-heart chats and got each other through some tough situations. He's a class act and will be a mate forever!

Ironically, my brother would be the same age as him if he were around today. His older brother is a big name in the Drum & Bass industry. Who is also a class bloke, that I am forever grateful toward, for his tutelage regarding my music. He is a big reason why I am making much better stuff today. Between him and Homegrown L. (Lauren) I have found my lane now and am very excited for future releases. Despite these positive encounters and messages, with many close friends. Things were still on rocky ground, so I ventured out into the woods alone for a wild camp. I planned it for Father's Day; as I thought that was a nice touch.

165

It was exhilarating to be alone in the woods, cut off from reality and the hustle and bustle of daily life. I thoroughly enjoyed myself, it's something I do regularly these days. I did have a slight dip in mental health around June; Tracey encouraged me go back to Hypnotherapy. I explained my external worries to Mrs. S and she said one sentence that changed my outlook on my situation. "What is meant for you won't go past you" I grabbed onto that saying, and I have held it as close to me as possible ever since. I need to remind myself of that from time to time. I tend to get a little complacent. Which I think we can all be guilty of now and then. After that Hypnotherapy session and some much-needed alone time in nature, I regained some stability. I was now able to regulate my peaks and troughs much easier than before.

I made a conscious decision to step away from alcohol. I didn't completely quit, but I gave up drinking unless I was going out on a rare occasion. Not only did that have a positive impact on my mental health, it helped my physique as well. I trained so hard and it seemed very counterproductive to drink. Even though I have never really been a heavy drinker, more of a binge drinker. It was dragging me down the day after. If I only had a few I'd wake up the next day with the beer fears, as they call it. I knew something was still missing from my life, I was on a roll and didn't want to let up. My writing was flying, and I was already piecing together my fourth album. The idea for the fifth was fully in motion. I was working on something else in the background, which is still a work in progress today. That is why I can't divulge what it is just yet. As it's something no one has ever done before. All I'll say is its lightly music based.

Things were looking measurably better, I just needed to find that missing link. September arrives, and I find myself in one of the most well-renowned Muay Thai gyms in the U.K. It was Martial Arts that was missing from my life. I feel complete again. I began to train twice a week and get that physical release I needed. With October on the doorstep, I am hoping and praying that nothing goes wrong again. Luckily, it flies by with no real hiccups. I'm in a good spot and striving forward. I have five albums wrapped up, written, sequenced, and named. I wrote one of them in around

166

two weeks; my sister didn't believe me. I was sending them quicker than she could bloody read them. All in all, I had bounced back once more and started to feel myself. I was in a battle; I wasn't about to lose!

I started to get a bit agitated about what to do for Christmas. I always feel filled with anxiety when it comes around, as I struggle with the fact I am technically alone. Tracey offers, which is lovely, but I always feel like I am imposing. Which I know is not true! Then, 15th of December, I am on a phone call to "The Advocate" She invites me round to hers with her family for Christmas. Fucking hell, I am welling up now whilst writing this. I am completely caught off guard, but I am elated! I ensured she was 100% sure; she said it would be lovely. Fighting back the tears, I graciously accept. How could I not? It turned out to be the best Christmas I have had in nearly a decade. I was so proud and honoured to be a part of it, with such a great bunch of people. It will forever stick in my memory. I'm quite a sentimental softy deep down, underneath all the darkness.

A week later. New Year's Eve, I'm with my mate Ross, seeing in the new year with him and his lovely, then-wife Rozzy, and his mum, who had basically adopted me. I wanted to keep my momentum going into 2023. I am now like a dog with a bone and can't wait to get going. First goal, as always. Keep mental health in check. January isn't off to a bad start. I am in a good place after a generally good year in 2022. I can't let up, I've got my goals to aim for, some of which are not hugely outlandish. I have just started putting in things on my list that aren't stressful to attain, to make it more fun. Although, I was about to be guided toward a path I never planned, or for one minute saw coming. 2023 looked a lot different than I could ever have imagined. I was on YouTube back In February at work, ironically sitting at the same computer I was when I discovered Miyamoto Musashi, on that day back in 2021.

I came across a video by a gentleman named Ryan Holiday. I had never heard of him before; the thumbnail and title piqued my curiosity. The video is called 12 Stoic Questions That Will Change Your Life. I wanted to be completely honest with myself on how many of these I could genuinely tick off the list. I ticked off 10 with confidence. There was one I was indifferent to. The other one needed a lot of work. eight years ago, I would have been lucky to tick off two. This is the original comment I posted on his YouTube page. "I've subbed as I feel you're going to help me get to where I'm trying to go. Great stuff!". Less than two hours after leaving this comment. I find myself enrolled on an online course in Stoicism & Philosophy. It said to allow for 150 hours to complete the course. I wanted to test myself on something I wasn't previously educated in and see if I could write something that wasn't in the format I am used to. I was never very academic in school, and English was something I struggled with regarding the technicalities. I seemed to be soaking up this information very quickly! I was so interested in the subject. It was extremely close to what I had already studied in Miyamoto Musashi. Which I found fascinating! I started the course on February 25th, I had it finished by March 3rd. I am not sure how I managed it so quickly. I just got addicted to it and was encapsulated by what I was reading, I couldn't put it down. As soon as I finished, I sent close friends and family a picture of the certificate. I sent some of them the actual diploma to read. Everyone was quite shocked as I never said a word. As soon as I had completed the course, I missed it. It was from that point on that Stoicism was to be a part of the rest of my life. It has reinforced what I am already doing and is a great addition to keeping my mental health in good shape. In the final Chapter, you will see how much it has affected my life.

Chapter 15

Philosophical Summary

I find it ironically hilarious that I am sitting here writing the last chapter of my book. For the kid whose parents were told their son would never walk or talk properly again. There's sheer dark humour and funny undertone in the fact that I went on to get a 2nd Dan Black Belt in kickboxing, be a musician, and become a writer. Whilst having a job where the main attribute is to possess good communication skills. All the things I shouldn't have been able to accomplish. Believe me, I didn't set out on this path deliberately. I am not looking for accolades or high praise, and I am not being braggadocios. Human beings have achieved amazing feats. I just wanted to flush this out from an almost third-person perspective and acknowledge it for what it is. Honestly, I find it quite funny! There's a tremendous amount of sullied water under the bridge of my turbulent life. All the things I have experienced have made me who I am today.

As I take stock of everything around me right now, I still can't help but feel a degree of disappointment and anguish. Don't get me wrong. I am happy I made it this far. I just often wonder if that unbreakable trust is something I'll find in someone. I'm not sure it exists although I want to be proved wrong. I spent two decades putting my hopes of love, trust, and happiness in others. Mainly women, if the truth be told. I don't think I am the only one guilty of this. But it is enlightening to think I could have been happier alone, rather than with the wrong person all these years and couldn't seem to grasp that notion. I suppose until you face yourself and accept who you were, who you are, and who you're trying to become, you're never going to have that self-realisation moment. I had no choice but to have that moment. It was also something I didn't fight. I know now that it was key for me to move on and be the man I was destined to become. I know there will be many forks in the road and important decisions to make to figure out what path I should take. Do we ever really know? Making the right decision is one of the toughest things to do in life. In my humble opinion, doing the right thing is rarely the easiest to do. Sometimes, it means cutting a part of yourself off to grow again. I'm not sure my heart can regenerate anymore. I have had parts cut off of me against my will many times, and I have severed some pieces of my heart myself. But, as one man famously said, "It wasn't the last straw that broke the camel's back. It was the million underneath it." I don't know how many more pieces I have to give, or break off from myself. That remains to be seen. I just hope there isn't a day where the last piece, is one I can never replace, and it all falls apart in front of my eyes. What might be the hardest thing to accept for any human being? Is that there's no permanence in anything? Everything that bleeds will die, and everything that's been built, will one day perish. I've been seven times down and eight times up. Those odds have to remain that way. It's not how many times you get knocked down to your knees; it's how many times you can rise. The only thing in this world you can solely rely on is yourself. Because once you realise that, then no one can beat you, or bring you down. You become the master of your own happiness.

Studying philosophy for the last year or so, has dramatically changed the outlook I have towards life. Seneca, Miyamoto Musashi, Geoff Thompson, Ryan Holiday, Epictetus, and Marcus Aurelius, all gave me uncut gems to build a new version of myself. It's all very well to quote these great men and say these words out loud, it's actioning these words that is the challenge. I know there's an incredible amount of work that needs to be done and I won't shy away from that fact. That is why I need to keep this in mind - stillness is key. My time comes above anything in this world, as we die every day. Yesterday is never coming back, and tomorrow, well, it isn't promised for you, me, or anyone else. I want to be able to shut my eyes at night and think that if I died in my sleep, then that was a great day I achieved x. y. and z. What astonishes me? The fact that we're all out here making plans for when we want to retire and how great our pension will be. We work all the hours God sends us. But we fail to realise Memento Mori. How ignorant and complacent can we be? I know that may ruffle a few feathers, but our grandiose plans do not exist! Only in our heads, and even then, why trouble our brains with these hypothetical pipe dreams? The rat race many of us are caught up in is one that I am not fully invested in, thankfully! Now, I'm not saying please don't have goals, dreams, or aspirations. That's simply not the case. What I am saying is, what about now? What about today? This minute you are basking in right now! The disregard, neglect, and almost contempt we harbour for the present moment as human beings is disturbing, to say the least. I may be coming across as hard-headed and a little preachy, but it is something I'd like everyone to honestly consider and note down. Nothing is more precious than the moment. The past breeds grief, the future breeds anxiety, and the present is a gift.

I have changed the way I now navigate my days, and that's to enjoy each part of my journey. The end goal isn't always a happy moment. You don't just become great at what you're working on overnight. Anything worth doing takes time and dedication. Sometimes blood, sometimes pain, sometimes tears, sometimes a broken heart, and sometimes grief. I have experienced them all, and I wish I didn't have that illustrious checklist. The media have done an exceptional job of making you believe what you should be doing, or what you need to acquire. From the latest phone, to the latest electric car, to a fancy holiday. It's all bullshit! The most solid of characters still need to step outside the box sometimes and have a look from a bird's-eye view. Nothing is really as it seems.

I find human life weird if I am being honest. The revolving door of procreation, to keep repeating this process and thinking they'll be a better tomorrow is the definition of madness, isn't it? Find a partner, buy a house, get married, have kids, get a better car, and then buy a bigger house. Then you have to work overtime to pay for all those things and not be on the bread line. So, the question I pose to you; Why do you focus on materialistic objects in your life and not focus on yourself? Could it be society has shaped

171

our ideals? There is no time like the present to recalibrate your focus and look inwards for personal development. I'm glad I'm not trapped in this never-ending cycle that's been laid out for us. I know what I want and who I am now. It's taken me up to the age of 40 to work that out. Most people have already done all of the aforementioned before their 30th birthday and have not had a chance to figure out who they really are or what they truly want from life. The whole "life begins at forty" line seems to make more sense now. I am not saying that, that life choice is inherently the wrong option. It's just that most of us don't understand what you signed up for, and by the time we do, some just go through the motions because that's what everyone else has done. It's all too late then, and you can't push your kids back or throw a tantrum about your mortgage being too dear and walk out and refuse to pay. You're locked in, and the only way out for some is ultimately suicide. Or winning the lottery, if you're lucky. Unfortunately, male suicide is something that has become more and more prevalent in the 21st century. I think it's blindingly obvious as to why that is, don't you? Many of us can't handle life, and there's no shame in that whatsoever! The weight of the expectation that rests on our shoulders is overbearing at the best of times. Men - society has made you think about what you should or have to do as a man. If you don't, you're weak and pathetic, and all these things that the uneducated readily bestow upon you to keep you in check and play the game.

Women. They're still being treated like they can't do as good a job in many fields, and unnecessarily so in many instances. I'd like to see those men in a cage with a female UFC fighter. Let's discuss the first round or when you wake up! I sit here in absolute stillness right now and am quite happy I decided to be the one playing Draughts while everyone else plays Chess. I will never let money be my driving force or let the innate pressure of society try to mould me into their ideals. I crave space, freedom, peace, love, enjoyment of life, and the time to make these things possible. Life ends at 25 for so many of us and if I die tomorrow, at least I have had some extra time.

I never thought I'd be here for a long time, but while I do exist in the physical, I want to have a good time and leave my mark on your hearts and souls. Not for my benefit, but for the benefit of others who will have to go on and be here. If one sentence, one song, or a moment we shared can leave a mark on you, then my work here is done. I will be more than happy with that. There's still so much I want to do, but I'd be the world's biggest hypocrite to think those things are guaranteed in the future. I'll just keep incrementally building each day and respecting the present moment in my journey. I will always hold onto the hope that I can achieve what I set out to do. Because without hope, what have we got?

Lately, I've been experiencing the most strange and unexplainable feelings. I feel like I'm in my second life, and that I've trod these paths before, and I'm sure I'll be here again one day. Things feel weird right now. It's as if there's a switch somewhere that someone has flicked; it's a switch that has a light on both ways you flick it. Either way, I'm going to be taken by the powers that be or I'm going to go on and change lives with my words. I would very much like it to be the latter of the two. Maybe this is just a caterpillar moment; I am shedding another skin and transforming into a better version of myself - one that'll go on to fly. Let's hope it's not just meandering towards the light without a cause or physical destination in mind.

Looking back at the years I so carelessly wasted in my twenties, I realise all too much how precious time is. You can never buy my time from me. Unless it's enough to free me from worry for the rest of my life, thus giving me more time to do the things I adore and look after the ones I cherish. There's this almost manic urgency I possess now in my daily life. It can be very exhausting, but it can also be rewarding. This is something I need to apply some temperance to. We are all marching towards death and that's just a fact of life. It doesn't scare me to die; it's more the fear of when it could happen - that's something none of us know. So, isn't it better to live each day like you might transition that night and embrace the fragility of our existence? Well, that's what I am going to do anyway, as I feel that way you have fewer regrets. Win the morning, and you'll win the day. Review it in the evening and see if what you've done during the day is worthy of being your last contribution to the planet.

It doesn't mean you have to do elaborate and noteworthy things every single day. It could be something very simple: making someone smile, helping someone with a problem, or offering solid advice to a loved one. But also saving a little in store for yourself in the process. Maybe start that project you keep pretending you don't have time for, or do that thing that petrifies you. You know deep down you are capable of it if you focus and put your mind to it. I will be taking my own advice on this and following up on the promise I made my dad all those years ago, by releasing my music, rather than just saying I will. To quote Seneca, "They lose the day in expectation of the night and the night in the fear of the dawn." I think that is a hugely relevant message today. Procrastination, we're all guilty of to a certain extent, me more so than anyone I know in the past; I almost think it's human nature at this point. Having the phrase Memento Mori close to my heart and soul at all times keeps me on my toes; I never get complacent, "we could leave right now." Honestly, let that rifle through your brain for a while, and then look at your kids, your wife, your mum or your dad. Tomorrow never comes! It may sound a bit depressing, but it is just a cold fact of life.

We can go on worrying about all the things none of us can control and wretch ourselves with unnecessary anxiety. To what avail? Who does that help? It's just better to embrace our fate. "Amor Fati": There is nothing more fruitless than fighting against what is naturally bestowed upon us. Unfortunately, those things aren't always good, getting angry or worrying about external events is as pointless as shouting at the paint on a wall to dry faster. I carried around grief and anger for most of my life; it got me nowhere but trouble and brought me and others pain, none of us needed. I wish I had this level of awareness before discovered that spending time alone in my inner sanctum was pivotal for my mental health years ago.

Being alone was one of my biggest fears back then, but now it takes someone very special to make me not want to be alone.

Although that's huge progress and ultimately much healthier, I also must be very diligent to not let that pendulum swing too far the other way. I don't want to completely cut myself off from my nearest and dearest; I just have to be selective with whom I spend time these days. I've never been so aware of how the people in your life can shape you. You are only as good as the company you keep, in most cases. I tend to surround myself with winners and fighters—people that inspire me. It's not that I need to gain anything from anyone, I'm Just mindful, if I surround myself with negative people who blame everything around them for their misfortunes, I'll find myself trapped in the same web they have woven. If I create my environment, I can only hold myself accountable for the things in my control.

Epictetus gave us some remarkable advice during his tenure. It's aged beautifully and will never not be relevant. I have embraced that advice wholeheartedly; it's a great tool to have in your box to help you maneuver through the tougher situations you could find yourself in at any moment. I'd highly recommend everyone doing this. Grab a piece of paper and draw a line down the middle. On the left-hand side, write at the top 'things in my control' and on the right 'things out of my control' a slightly different approach to my previous list. We can't control others' actions, deaths, traffic, weather, delayed flights, others' feelings, etc. Being angry or upset about something we have zero power or control over is only detrimental to our mental well-being, is it not? It will take me many more years to nullify and beat these external worries. It will be a long and arduous process; it is one I have to embark on and overcome to be truly at peace with myself.

The main ones on my list that are the toughest to tackle; being hopelessly in love with someone who doesn't feel the same or conceding that you can't take others' pain away. I'm not sure whether I'll ever be able to accept some of these external worries, that are out of my control. But I won't stop trying, as I know acceptance is the key. I can't be deluded enough and just sit around hoping that it will magically change, as I honestly don't think it ever will. The other stuff I can take in my stride and flip into positives. If I am ever stuck in traffic, I can put an instrumental on and practice some rhyming, or I can think of new ideas for my next album. Or call that person I haven't spoken to in ages and make sure they're okay. If it's raining, then I'll write a journal, a book, or a new track and train indoors that day. If grief strikes me unexpectedly, I won't react to the instant emotion; I'll sit down, take a deep breath, and figure out my next move as calmly as possible. Much easier said than done, I know; it is all trial and error, and I think I have experienced enough through my short time here so far to stand me in good stead for future events.

I regularly ask myself what it would be like without certain people in my life, and it breaks my heart. I have lost so many; I can't bear to think of losing more. But that's the reality, unfortunately. This philosophical outlook I now have on the world, makes me feel better equipped to deal with hardship. I am not saying I won't cry when someone passes or when someone fades out of my life forever! However, I will, in time, see it for what it is and realise I can only adapt to that particular moment as and when the time arises. I've decided to use the four Stoic virtues every day from this moment on. They are justice, temperance, courage, and wisdom. These four virtues will counter whatever comes my way. Justice is something I possess, but I had to do a lot of internal work and soul searching. Temperance, I need to do a lot of work on. I get locked into projects and hobbies so much that I lose myself and burn my brain out to the point where I am completely exhausted! Courage has been something I have had since a very young age. I had no choice; if I didn't have it, I wouldn't be writing these words right now. Finally, wisdom. I feel it's something I acquire day by day, and it comes more with age. I never thought I'd enjoy life as much as I do today; it is precious and beautiful, yet fleeting and fragile.

When I look back at that troubled 12-year-old boy, the teenage addict, and the broken man in his twenties living for the weekend and wishing life away. The lost soul that buried his head in drugs and alcohol, hoping that all the pain would just disappear if he got high and drunk enough. It's almost hard to believe that was

176

me. I hated that version of me, and I apologise to anyone who had the misfortune of experiencing it. That man was very weak and living in complete denial. I tried every way possible to escape what was going on around me. You can be sitting on the most idyllic beach in the world, on the precipice of a picturesque mountain, or looking across an empty field of nothing but nature in all its beauty, but you can't run away from your mind. If you're not happy and haven't dealt with what needs attention. It does not matter what scenery you surround yourself with, if the person inside is shattered and full of anguish. If you're truly happy, you can be happy in a traffic jam on the way home from work or standing in torrential rain at a bus stop on a Sunday evening.

I am now in a position to help those around me, more so from a supportive standpoint. When I was homeless, no one deserted me, thought I was a loser, or cut me off. Everyone stuck by me, and that's how I know I have real mates. One of the most well-aged statements my dad made all those years ago was. "When you get to my age, you can count your real friends on one hand." I am nowhere near the age my dad was when he told me that, I still can't use all ten fingers to count those friends. Quality over quantity is viable where that's concerned. Even though I spend much less time with my friends these days, that's not all down to me. That's life in general; it happens to the best of us and with age comes more responsibility. I am an extremely busy man, it's a busy life that I welcome not to endure. I do make moments for self-reflection, no matter how painful that can be sometimes. I go for long walks across the fields in my local area. Nothing makes me happier than the peace and tranquility that it has to offer; it is also time for me to dig deep within myself and bring some harder thoughts to the surface. I don't let it ruin my time alone outside in the wilderness, but I do flush out some painful external worries to combat them. Once I arrive back home, I don't pretend I have "fixed" them, but I know I took another step towards stopping them from overwhelming me. Each day is a challenge and part of the process. The bigger picture can't be painted with a single brush stroke. Mental health is like a broken cup or an oil leak on your motorcycle. It can't put itself back together, or close up on its own accord to be permanently fixed. But it is like a flower, one that needs watering daily to stay in good health. The mistake I; and I am sure many others have made before, is that when you get to a "good place." You think okay, I'm all better now, and forget how you got there and, more importantly, how the fuck you are going to remain there.

The only predictable thing is unpredictability; you cannot afford to rest on your laurels when you've experienced trauma. It's a sad fact; working on yourself is a job that never reaches completion. You have to accept that, because once you do, you stop chasing that unattainable moment like a crazed greyhound chasing Rusty the rabbit he's never going to catch. I will continue to read the 21 Rules of Life by Miyamoto Musashi every day and study Stoicism. I have other coping mechanisms that come in the forms of literature and visual. You are best served to do what works for you; there's no right or wrong answer. "Conquer your grief; don't deceive it." You can hide from pain, you can run from trauma, and you can stifle your inner demons. But one day, they will knock on your door. Guess what? You will be in! I've seen the strongest break in front of my own eyes. Don't think it won't happen to you, because every day has its dawn and every human has a tipping point.

To think you are exempt from such a thing is true delusion and ignorance. It takes a real man to cry and ask for help; it takes a fool to suffer in silence. Take it from the biggest fool going. Me! I advocate balancing physical and mental activities in your life. If you can unload your brain and body weekly, you will find yourself in a place of inner contentment. For example, I have physical and mental outlets in writing and music, as well as martial arts and calisthenics. For which I am very grateful, but it doesn't matter what you do. You could go for a run or paint a picture. This is great self-therapy and keeps the body functioning the way it should. If I could choose one bit of information for everyone who reads this book to make a habit of, it would be to write a list. Not on your phone - on a piece of paper. You know, like we used to - write a short list of goals or things you want for the next year. They don't have to be lofty or overly grandiose. Maybe one or two of them could be just make sure they're realistic and fully attainable. For example, 'I want to pass my driving test this year.' That's a big one; the next one could be 'I want to get fit' or 'I want to get that tattoo I have wanted for the last couple of years. These things are realistic and feel-good goals. This may sound contradictory to what I have said before about making plans, as we don't know what can happen in life. These goals are more immediate and something you can get to work on right away! However, the goal 'I want to have paid off my mortgage by the time I am 55 years old and be sitting on a beach in Hawaii,' sounds good, but realistically is two or three decades away for many. Being brutally honest, I have always found that incredibly strange - why wait for the last quarter of your life to start living? The aches and pains of a senior years will be encroaching upon you, and you'll be much less able-bodied than you are right now.

I have learned the hard way through my catalogue of errors; one thing that strangely has been my worst downfall is also my best attribute - an addictive personality! If you direct it through the right channels, it can bring some amazing things into your life. I was addicted to certain drugs for many years. That brought me nothing but heartache and misery. Now, I'm addicted to writing, music, training, etc. Regardless of whether it's positive or not. I can zone in on things I am working on and unequivocally demand the best from myself without exception. I used to pride myself on being the last man standing on a Saturday night; now I pride myself on being the best at my craft. My passions are my life force and what keeps me ticking. I am starting to practice gratitude much more diligently and am reminding myself that it is the little things in this world that matter most.

The best things in life are free; they cost energy and time. That's ok if that time and energy are well spent. People readily give out time like leaflets and won't buy you a beer. I'd give all the time in the world to someone if they deserved it, and I'd buy them beers all night, despite the lack of gratitude some have shown over the years. I don't let it deter me from helping good people. Past experiences can make you bitter and poisonous. I have seen it; it pushes people away very quickly. An ex-girlfriend of mine possessed this trait and despite all my best efforts to please her, I was just another horrible man who would eventually do her wrong. If you expect the worst from everyone, they'll never be able to give you, their best. I prepare for the worst and expect the best nowadays. I wear my heart on my sleeve and am an extremely passionate person, much to my detriment sometimes. Probably the Leo in me. Knee-jerk reactions are sometimes my weakness. I am trying hard to internalise before I vocalise, no matter how testing the circumstance is.

A part of being a Stoic is to not get emotional or overly excited. Unfortunately, for me, I can be both of those things. It's not that I want to completely change who I am. I am, who I am. That should be embraced and nurtured, not disregarded. But there is a time and a place for both of those things and sometimes a little decorum goes a long way. The last 18 months have been a huge learning curve and almost a test of character. I want nothing but the best for great people. Not everything is about me and my feelings; it's about the person or people I love. I thought I knew what true love was, but I was sorely mistaken and had the most basic grasp on it. I have proven to myself that I can love someone as they should and deserve to be loved, regardless of whether they love me back. Although my last two relationships were disastrous, it hasn't made me resentful or vengeful. I have made inner peace with my past, as I have had to for my own good. I am the happiest I have been in years! I think that is down to an amalgamation of different things—being surrounded by the right people. Show me who your friends are, and I'll show you where you'll be in five years. I'm finally living a life that has a sense of direction and a feeling of contentment, which I had been lacking for so many years in my past. I know there is a cobbled road of uncertainty that lies before me and all I can do is do my best to tread it thoughtfully and carefully from this point on.

Now that I don't waste energy on anything that's not necessary, I find I have a lot more in the tank to use up on things I genuinely love and enjoy. I also recognise the warning signs for when my mental health starts to take a dip. I don't let myself go into the abyss now and wallow in the mire of anxiety; I take a step back and try to self-assess why I am feeling the way I am. My brain is a tough place to be sometimes; it will go off on its little journey quite regularly. I have to really drag it back and bring it back under my control. I'll shamelessly quote the great Seneca again, as I don't think this particular quote could ever be said enough. "We suffer more often in our imagination than in reality." I am the world's biggest offender where that is concerned; it is something I will forever be working on. I'm aware of this and will get better at it as time passes. I know that's one for the long haul, though. Most of my troubles and inner woes came from trying to seek validation from others. I thought if someone loved me, that would make me feel better and answer my insecurities. Hence why I kept regressing and failing to move forward. I am not searching for the "ideal" life and trying to make everything perfect! Because nothing will ever be that way. I will continue to follow this path, live in the best way I can, and honor my family, despite most of them being on another plane. Now that I know they can send messages to me and vice versa, it's only right that I live my life with justice. I'm not going to pretend I am going to be this perfect man, a hero wearing a cape who never does any wrong at all. I'll just make sure I remain the best version of myself and make tiny improvements each day. I vowed nearly a decade ago that I would never touch drugs again. I said if I did, I'd throw myself off a building. I meant it! I could never go back to being that guy. It is a shadow of the man I am today. I would like to take this moment to apologise properly to anyone I hurt on my journey. Please realise that there was no intention behind my actions, I was just another lost soul burying his head in drugs and alcohol. What is done is done; I can't go back and right those wrongs. All I can do is do better from now on.

I would like to share a verse I heard last year that sums up how I feel, about who I used to be and the regrets I have. I've written many lyrics, but I'm not sure any of them could top these from Styles P: *"Tried in the fire, it never burned my flesh. May I learn my lessons? May I learn my steps? May I indulge in the dirt? Yeah, I earned my mess, and I hurt a lot of people. I deserve my stress. I showed a lot of people my worst who preferred my best."* I think that says it perfectly! Unfortunately, once a man built on sand dunes and pessimism, is now slowly becoming a man built on concrete foundations full of stoicism and belief. All I've ever known is pain, but it's made me stronger than your average person. I can't help but fight; that's all I know how to do, and I can't throw the towel in now; I'm only in the 6th round. I'll die in this ring if I have to. So, I'll bite down on this gum shield and take the metaphorical kicks, punches, elbows, and knees that life will inevitably keep throwing at me. I won't shell up and hope it'll stop, as that's unlikely. My dad taught me that no matter how bad things get, you always have fight left. If he fought for twelve years with cancer, then I can fight through my pain as well. There's not much of an excuse, and I wouldn't want to turn up at the pearly gates early and get a slap from him!

Don't get me wrong; sometimes I still look at that pull-up bar and think, I could do that, you know. As I have been frighteningly close to turning my lights out before, I know I can do it. But that makes me not want to. I meditate on the thoughts of all the people left in my wake and see the pain in their eyes. I couldn't do it to them; I would rather be in pain and live through it, than make them pay for my waves of unhappiness. In general, I'm okay these days. I have my moments, as everyone does, but it's not dark enough for me to move on. I have to remember why I am here and what I have left to do. That in itself will give me the fuel I need to go on. I am ultra-mindful of the signs now; I got this! In the words of the almighty legend, Miyamoto Musashi, "Never stray from the way".
There has been a massive part of me lately that wants to move and start a whole life away from Kent. Maybe even the UK. But I can't do it; there are too many people I love nearby, and that's not the answer. Plus, I have all I need right here. I know what I need to do more often, and that's get out in nature and enjoy life. Wild camping is a therapy that I need. I grew up living right next to the woods and I feel at peace there. Free from my busy city job. I'm grateful for my job, but London is a manic place and I find it taxing on my body and mind. It's taken me too long to figure out how I can function as a "normal" human being. I take my rest when I need to and I work relentlessly when I know I'm in the right mindset. I just have to be cautious of my thoughts, and up and down moments.

There was a while when my sister Tracey thought I was bipolar. My highs and lows were extreme! When I did my due diligence on that disorder, I nearly convinced myself to be honest. After weathering that storm, I realised it was just a moment of instability that was prevalent in my life at the time. I was on trembling ground and experiencing unrelenting spikes of emotion. That has made me a creature of habit, and I'm being introspective here. If I get shaken out of my routine, I notice I'm not as content as when I'm in it. Lately, I've been more flexible and starting to be much less stringent in how I go about each week. Now, I rarely think more than two days ahead if I can help it. It doubles back on not letting external events affect my daily life. It's helping me be more adaptable to 90% of situations. I'm not foolhardy enough to think my life will follow this perfect linear trajectory from this point on. Staying on top of things is paramount and no one else is going to do it for me. It's all about stepping outside the box and looking at yourself now and then. Sometimes I have been very guilty of being ignorant to my problems and sinking into darkness! That still scares me a bit to this day, as when I go to that place, no one can save me. It's really hard to drag myself out of those doldrums. Although, this rarely happens now. I am much better at nullifying it before it gets too bad; I can't always achieve that, though. Now, when I get that cold feeling of pins and needles rushing like a tidal wave up my body, it doesn't drag me down, or death roll me like a crocodile of anxiety.

I'm fully aware that many moments in this book may have been hard to read for some. Some might be feeling sorry for me, and shocked about who I used to be and the fact that I still struggle quite a lot even today. I don't want any of those emotions from anyone. I wrote this book for a few reasons. The first was in the hope that I could help someone else who has suffered trauma and has mental health issues. If one person comes up to me one day and says, I read your book, and it helped me through the dark patch. That would be enough for me. Secondly, I wanted to see if I could do this sort of thing. I have written lyrics for years; that has been my wheelhouse for so long. After completing the Diploma in Stoicism and Philosophy early on in 2023, it breathed a new lease of life into me. I realised I love writing, regardless of what format it might be in. Thirdly, so many of my friends have witnessed my journey and have said many things to me. One of which being, "You should write a book, mate!" So, here it is. I am not interested in the money or the fame; I never have been. Whether you believe it or not, I do this purely for love and self-therapy, and as aforementioned, to hopefully help someone else through stuff they may be going through. While I bring up the subject of money and fame, if you have kindly purchased this book, firstly, thank you so much for the support. I wouldn't be here if it weren't for so many of you who have helped me through. I'd also like to take this moment to thank "The Advocate" for being a huge reason I made it through some incredibly dark times. You pop up like an angel so much. This book wouldn't look like it does without your help. I love you! And lastly, my one-of-a-kind sister, Tracey; without her, I'd be dead! That's not hyperbole in any way, shape, or form. She has been a sister, a mum, a friend, a therapist, and the rock I still often lean on today. I feel for her because she's spent most of her life clearing up the mess of others. She had her own family to raise and still kept ours together for so long. Dad would have died at least 5 years prior without her selflessness and dedication to helping him.

The one good thing that can come from hardship is that it can make bonds stronger! Weirdly, Tracey sometimes rings me for help and advice. Which is nice, but I don't think I'll ever get used to it. I'm glad that I can help her make a change. No matter how many times I help her, I can never repay her. Not only has she saved my life, but she also raised two great children and has been the foundation of the family unit. Not just ours, but her own. There are not enough words available to do her justice and thank her for the life she let me have. You would never know in a million years what she has been through herself. My sister is the life and soul of any party; you know, when she's in a room, she gets that trait from my dad. So, sis, thank you for saving me; I'm forever in your debt. I love you so much! Thank you for helping me so much with this book. I needed it!

For all the people that were there for my lowest points and saw my worst. It's my time to repay you. If any of you need me, I am here! So, to all the people in my life, I truly thank you from the bottom of my heart. I am going to end on this positive note, one that I hope sticks with you all. Just remember, wherever you are, whatever you are doing, and whatever things are simmering in your brain, you've got options... I'm going to leave some coping mechanisms I use to help my mental health. Here are some books, quotes, and videos for you all to watch when life gets a bit much. Not all of these things will work for everyone, as we're all different. Pick the bones out of what serves you best. Horses for courses, as they say. Firstly, I'd like to recommend my coping strategies for those darker days. If you start to dip and feel that sense of impending doom, get up immediately from where you are, go and pour a glass of water, put the TV. on, clear a drawer out, run the hoover around... Anything! This may sound completely bonkers, but trust me, it works. It is an immediate distraction from what is on your mind at that moment. Then I'd recommend going for a walk, chucking some music on, and getting out in nature. Find a field, some woods, somewhere quiet. If there's no place like this where you live, travel somewhere. Go camping or hiking. Take your head out of social media for a while; that is the most toxic place you could wish to be in the world. The day I deleted it was the day my mental health got measurably better. A true lifesaver - have hobbies! I can't stress this enough. Make sure they're things you can do on your own that you genuinely enjoy. Whether that's physical or mental activity, it doesn't matter. It's best if you have both. Plan one day at a time, and don't get overwhelmed with thoughts of a future that doesn't exist. Just be present. If you're in turmoil over your past, like I have been, ask yourself what will feeling like that change? Accept that you are just a human being, nothing more, nothing less. We have all messed up! Don't hate who you were; just be better today and don't make those same errors again. That's the remedy. Have a morning ritual—something that takes no longer than 20 minutes, so it is sustainable to do every day. My ritual consists of reading the 21 rules of life by Miyamoto Musashi, and 15 minutes meditation.

One video I would like to share with everyone, which I watch for inspiration 5 or 6 times a year is Retrain Your Mind – Joe Rogan, you'll find it on YouTube. The Mulligan Brothers channel. It's well worth 18 minutes of your time. Another good strategy, which I am not currently doing myself, as I tend to get most of my daily inner thoughts out via my music - Keep a journal. It's a powerful tool that many have used and swear by. Flush your thoughts out for the day, write down what's bothered you and/or what you want to improve on. Keep track of your mental health as well. It's basically like tracking your workouts. But for the mind instead of the body.

The books I would recommend are:

Seneca's 'The Shortness of Life',
Miyamoto Musashi's 'The Book of Five Rings',
Seneca's 'Letters from a Stoic',
Marcus Aurelius 'Meditations',
Geoff Thompson 'The Elephant and the Twig'
Epictetus 'The Discourses'.

These books, I guarantee, will answer some, if not all your questions and give you some clarity moving forward. Here are some quotes you can expect to find in the books I have listed. I hope they will be enough to encourage you to pick at least one of them up and have a read:

Epictetus - "It's not what happens to you, but how you react to it that matters".

Marcus Aurelius - "The happiness of your life depends on the quality of your thoughts".

Seneca - "Sometimes just to live is an act of courage".

Miyamoto Musashi - "Think lightly of yourself and deeply of the world".

Ok, I'm signing out! Don't forget to love yourself, accept everything just the way it is, get some time alone, enjoy life, "don't make a promise you can't keep, don't make a keepsake out of grief" and above all, "Amor Fati" and "Memento Mori".

P.S. Before it's your final roll of the dice. Just remember, it's only all over when you no longer fight.

Ronnie D Stevens 2024.

Milton Keynes UK
Ingram Content Group UK Ltd.
UKHW032322121024
449589UK00010B/403